from Present to Future

Catholic Education in Ireland
for the New Century

Edited by Eithne Woulfe & James Cassin

VERITAS

First published 2006 by
Veritas Publications
7/8 Lower Abbey Street
Dublin 1
Ireland

Email publications@veritas.ie
Website www.veritas.ie

ISBN 1 85390 903 3
978 1 85390 903 0 (from January 2007)

10 9 8 7 6 5 4 3 2 1

Andrew G. McGrady's 'The Religious Dimension of Education in Irish Second-Level Schools at the Start of the Third Millennium' was originally published in the Religious Education Annals in *Religion, Education and the Arts* (REA), Issue 4, published by Mater Dei Institute of Education, 2003.

Joseph Dunne's 'The Catholic School, the Democratic State and Civil Society: Exploring the Tensions' was originally published in *The Catholic School in Contemporary Society*, papers presented at a conference on 19–21 April, 1991, published by the Conference of Major Religious Superiors (Ireland), Dublin, 1991.

The lines from Patrick Kavanagh's 'Why Sorrow' are reprinted from *Patrick Kavanagh: The Complete Poems* (Newbridge, 1972, 1984) by kind permission of the Trustees of the Estate of the late Katherine B. Kavanagh, through the Jonathan Williams Literary Agency.

Excerpts from 'Missing God' are taken from *Dennis O'Driscoll: New and Selected Poems*, published by Anvil Press Poetry in 2004, used with permission.

Scripture quotations from the *New Revised Standard Version Bible* © 1993 and 1998 by the Division of Christian Education of the National Council of the Churches of Christ in the United States of America.

Printed in the Republic of Ireland by Betaprint Ltd, Dublin

Veritas books are printed on paper made from the wood pulp of managed forests. For every tree felled, at least one tree is planted, thereby renewing natural resources.

Contents

Introduction

'His was the unusual ability to involve others in his work for the Church',[1] writes the late historian Donal Kerr of Daniel Murray, coadjutor Bishop of Dublin (1809–1823), and its Archbishop until 1852. One wonders, what if Murray had not supported the emergence of religious communities that went on to provide educational and health services? What if Archbishop Murray or his successor Cardinal Cullen and the majority of their fellow bishops had opposed the State-sponsored National School system introduced in 1831? Indeed, it was opposed by some, including Archbishop McHale of Tuam, who preferred an independent Catholic school sector; separate from that of the State-sponsored system until after Independence. More than a century later, what if the bishops and religious had stalled the introduction of mass post-primary education in 1967 by not accepting the terms of the 'Free Education' scheme for Catholic secondary schools, and so making available (with few exceptions) secondary school buildings and facilities? Later again, agreements followed about the State's and Churches' interests in the development of comprehensive and community schooling.

Certain constants inform this story through changing contexts and times: evangelisation; episcopal mission in the creation of right pastoral structures for the people; the tension between charism and institutional needs; enormous investment by dioceses and religious in schooling provision and maintenance; vision of Catholic education, Irish Catholic identities; the contribution of education in alleviating poverty and enhancing dignity; pragmatism in tune with the political reality of the day[2] and adaptation to changing needs; role of religious and the laity; joint Church–State investment in schools; and the ever-lurking question of the desirability and effectiveness of schools being a dominant locus of evangelisation on this island. The inheritance and decisions of yesteryear have been and continue to be defining instances. They also prompt key questions for the decision makers and shapers of educational opportunity in the twenty-first century. What if … ?

It is hoped that the papers now being published in this volume, *From Present to Future: Catholic Education in Ireland for the New Century,* will be a contribution to ongoing discernment and planning. The papers were presented in February 2005 at a two-day conference jointly organised by the Education Commissions of the Irish Episcopal Conference and the Conference of Religious in Ireland (CORI). The conference was designed for the Bishops and Leaders of Religious Congregations in their role as Ordinaries of dioceses and Trustees of Catholic schools to discuss the issue 'Catholic Education in Contemporary Ireland'. Other guests were in attendance in the context of their representing pivotal interests for Catholic education in Ireland.

In his welcoming address, Bishop Leo O'Reilly of the Irish Bishops' Commission for Education said:

> The significant achievements of Catholic education can be seen all around us in the Ireland of today. However, the critical task now for all committed to sustaining a Catholic ethos in the educational system is to confidently

reassert this agenda in order to construct a sustainable model for the benefit of future generations. For this to work, lay ownership of such a model is vital. Complacency is not an option. We must face head-on today's challenges to Catholic education. The tradition that brought us to this point will not continue if we do not act responsibly. We must adapt to the changing circumstances of modern Ireland. The purpose of this inter-conference meeting is to enable all of us (the Trustees of Catholic schools) to consider – in collaboration – our current circumstances so that we can start to plan and develop policies guaranteeing the future of our schools. The two-day meeting is part of a process that will, over the coming months, evaluate the Catholic education system in terms of its characteristic spirit, commitment to formation, academic achievement, trusteeship, inclusion, diversity, as well as other core elements.

Bishop O'Reilly concluded:

Historically, the delivery of Catholic education has been characterised by pro-activity and quality service. However, current and future social circumstances are radically different to the education needs of people in a bygone era. We must reassess our ability both to meet sufficiently the needs of our people and fulfil our mission in terms of education. It is, therefore, time to plan for the future.

The conference was attended by Archbishop Michael Miller CSB of the Roman Congregation for Catholic Education and Rev. Henry Lemoncelli OMI of the Roman Congregation for Institutes of Consecrated Life and for Societies of Apostolic Life, who addressed the conference from the perspective of the universal Church. Four Irish guest speakers addressed a number of the key issues central to the contemporary Catholic education system in Ireland and the challenges facing it in the future. This afforded bishops and congregational leaders the opportunity to engage together with the current reality in Ireland, from the perspective of Church, education, law, policy, theology and trusteeship. Thus, changes in the culture, in society and in the Church – which have an impact on the Church and education profile – were raised. The process used included small group and plenary discussions. These discussions were directed and informed by five papers which were commissioned for the conference. The major themes emerging from the papers and the discussions were identified and synthesised throughout the conference.

The conference concluded its deliberations by recommending the establishment of a Strategic Task Group for Education to bring forward, as a matter of urgency, the recommendations from the conference. This task group would work in the context of a 'One Church' commitment to and a strategic plan for the provision and development of Church interests in education. This work is ongoing at the time of writing.

This book contains the texts of five papers presented at the conference, as well as the homily of the Apostolic Nuncio. These papers appear in the form in which they were given by the authors. The book also contains two additional papers, which have already been published elsewhere and which complement the conference papers.

David Tuohy SJ, an academic and educational consultant both nationally and internationally, is the author of the first paper, 'Issues in Catholic Education in Ireland'. This paper explores a number of contested areas related to Catholic schools and their future: the understanding of 'Catholic', and the purpose of schooling. These considerations lead to a third area – the attempts to integrate these two areas in a Catholic school and the ensuing challenges and possibilities.

'The Trusteeship of Catholic Schools' was written by Mary Reynolds RSM, a member of the Central Leadership Team of the Congregation of the Sisters of Mercy (Ireland). Her paper traces the growing awareness among Religious Congregations in Ireland of the meaning of active trusteeship. Sr Mary reminded conference members that Religious congregations in their exploration of 'new forms of trusteeship' are not in the mindset of 'closing down' but rather of passing on something that they have pioneered and developed: 'This time has great possibilities within it for empowerment of laity, collaboration among Religious Congregations and Explorations with Bishops, who hold ultimate responsibility for Catholic education, and also it offers above all the opportunity to revise and revitalise the Catholic school and education with contemporary Irish society, as a contribution to the common good in a new Ireland.' Suggestions about possible new structures for the exercise of trusteeship by the laity, including the creation of an Association of the Christian Faithful and the empowerment of the laity by the recognition of trusteeship as ministry in the Church, are addressed.

'The Ecclesial Dimension of Catholic Education' was written by Archbishop J. Michael Miller CSB, Secretary, Congregation for Catholic Education. An educational leader in North America for twenty years before his translation to the Congregation, Archbishop Miller reiterated certain constant elements about the specific ethos of Catholic schools which the Church proposes in her teaching. Like the marks of the Church proclaimed in the Creed, he identifies the principal 'ideal' characteristics of a school *qua Catholic*. In so doing, he expands the four ecclesial marks to five scholastic ones. Catholic schools proceed *ex corde Ecclesiae*, from the very heart of the Church, both universal and local.

Professor John Coolahan, Professor Emeritus of Education at the National University of Ireland, Maynooth, addressed the issue of 'Church, State and Education in Contemporary Ireland:

Some Perspectives'. In the current context of a demonstratively new historical era of educational change, Professor Coolahan briefly reviews three periods: (i) Church and State pre-1922 – the period of the Church winning control of education; (ii) the first four decades after Independence, which he terms as the Church maintaining control in education; (iii) more recent decades in the contemporary period where the Church is increasingly sharing control in education. He posits that the enormously changing contemporary educational canvas with its burgeoning focus on technology, and life-long as distinct from school-based learning, offers both challenge and hope to society, the State and the Church.

'Challenges facing Catholic Education in Ireland' is the title of Dr Dermot Lane's paper. A priest of the Dublin Archdiocese, President of Mater Dei Institute of Education, Dublin City University, and parish priest of Balally, he is a writer and teacher of systematic theology. His paper offers a description of recent developments in education, an analysis of some of the cultural changes within contemporary Ireland, a critique of developments in higher education and concludes with concrete proposals for the future. He stresses the critical need for congruence between school ethos and the content of religious education, together with the need for critical reflection and conversation within the syllabi themselves. He strongly posits the case for life-long learning and the place of theology and spirituality therein.

The final two papers did not constitute presentations at the conference but are included as it was felt that they served to complement the papers presented and would facilitate further consideration and discussion on the issues raised by the guest speakers at the conference.

'The Religious Dimension of Education in Irish Second-Level Schools at the Start of the Third Millennium' by Dr Andrew G. McGrady, Registrar of Mater Dei Institute of Education, was originally published in the Religious Education

Annals in *Religious Education and the Arts* (REA), Issue 4, Mater Dei Institute of Education. The author articulates six essential dimensions of the Catholic school. He suggests that any specific approaches to implementing these six general dimensions for Catholic schools in Ireland must move from seeing such schools as isolated entities or institutions to seeing them as embedded communities, the nature and purpose of which depend upon a clear understanding of other related factors and contexts. Catholic schools are embedded in a wider ecclesial framework, in a partnership framework with parents, teachers and other social partners, and they are embedded within a wider constitutional, legal, economic and socio-cultural framework. The shape of these wider frameworks determines the specific identity and purpose of Catholic schools in Ireland with the broad umbrella of the six religious dimensions of education.

'The Catholic School, the Democratic State and Civil Society: Exploring the Tensions', written by Joseph Dunne, a lecturer in philosophy in St Patrick's College, Dublin City University, was originally published in *The Catholic School in Contemporary Society* – papers presented at a conference in 1991. The author, in agreeing to have his paper included in this volume (with expanded title) wishes it to be pointed out that, as a paper written fifteen years ago, it addresses none of the significant subsequent developments, including the 1998 Education Act. His paper examines some key philosophical ideas, such as 'ethos', that are implicit in the concept of the Catholic school. He also explores some significant tensions derived from the insertion of Catholic schools in a contemporary pluralist society.

The homily delivered by the Apostolic Nuncio, Archbishop Giuseppe Lazzarotto at the conference is included in the publication. The conference brought together a spectrum of interests within the Catholic world of education from the local to the national and universal. The presence of His Excellency, the Apostolic Nuncio, together with delegates of two Roman congregations, Archbishop Miller and Father Lemoncelli, symbolised the universal nature of Catholic education and schools.

This conference raised a number of long-term implications for Catholic education in Ireland. These have not yet been explored. It has been decided not to further develop the themes raised in this volume. This is for another time. By refraining from doing so, it is hoped that readers will ask their own questions, listen to their musings and, when the time comes, enable their informed responses to the questions which might begin with 'what if ... ?'. Only thus will new futures emerge.

Many people, other than those who presented papers, helped to bring this conference to fruition and to make the present publication possible. Dr Johanna Merry facilitated the conference. Members of the Columba Centre and CORI Secretariats, Helen Reynolds, Breda Murphy, Eithne Barry and Noreen Kennedy, were involved in the administration of the conference. Special appreciation goes to the participants who, by their attendance and wholehearted engagement, gave life to the proceedings. These proceedings have since led to further dialogue and engagement with a wider audience, a process that it is hoped will continue. May this publication too enable an ever-widening audience to engage in the process initiated at this February 2005 Conference – a first in Irish history!

James Cassin
Eithne Woulfe
July 2006

Notes

1 'Murray, prudent and cautious though he was, welcomed anyone who had something useful to do for the diocese and the people of Dublin. Always willing to help and advise, he was reluctant to interfere.' Kerr, in *The Catholic Archdiocese of Dublin*, Dublin: Veritas, 2000, p. 255.

2 E. Doyle, *Leading the Way*, Secretariat of Secondary Schools, Dublin, 2000.

Homily of
Archbishop Giuseppe Lazzarotto
Apostolic Nuncio

Maynooth, 7 February 2005

(Gen 1:1-19; Mk 6:53-56)

The text from Genesis, with which we began this ceremony, introduces us to God's creative work – a work that continues to amaze us with its greatness, its harmony and beauty. It also lays claim to our responsibility, because it is to each one of us that God entrusts his creation; we are the ones who are asked to preserve it and bring it to perfection.

The great task of 'educating', to which you will be dedicating time and attention during these days of reflection, is certainly one of the highest and noblest ways we have of responding to the task that God set us when he placed his creation in our hands.

I have no ambition to touch upon the subject matter of the discussions you will have during this conference – there are eminent specialists here to do just that. I warmly congratulate, however, the promoters of this timely initiative and I have no doubt that the strands of reflection that you will be teasing out during this meeting will be of great service not alone to all the participants but also to all those with whom you will later share your findings. It is paramount, of course, that in your reflections due space be given to the families who entrust their children to your care, to the teachers who play a fundamental role in education and to all those who are engaged in the irreplaceable task of educating the younger generations. It is truly a concerted task that calls for our best efforts and our full commitment.

At this moment, we are invited to focus our attention on the word of God and to draw inspiration from it as we seek to understand the nature and demands of the educational task we are called upon to fulfil. It is quite natural that we should think of Jesus, the Son of God made man, who surrenders himself fully to the educational endeavours of Mary and Joseph and who, thanks to their care and attention, 'increased in wisdom, in stature and in favour with God and with people' (Lk 2:52).

This truly represents the 'complete education' of the person towards which should tend all those resources that the Church, in response to the command of her founder, dedicates to the task of education.

Returning again to our text from Genesis, I am reminded of a reflection of St Augustine in his commentary on Psalm 41: 'Where is your God? I too have sought my God so as to be able, not alone to believe in him, but also to try, as far as my strength will allow, to behold him … I see, indeed, the works of my God, but I do not see my God who has made all these things … I look at the heavens and the beauty of the stars … I admire the splendour of the sun and the moon that dispels the darkness of night. These beauties fill us with astonishment, they disconcert us, they lead us to meditate. Yet they do not satisfy my thirst: I admire it all, I praise it, but I thirst for the one who has created it.'

I sometimes see in the evening, as I look from the windows of the Nunciature or as I travel through the city, numerous groups of pupils on their way home from school, dressed in their uniforms, and I cannot but ask what seeds are being sown in their minds and hearts through the education they are getting in our many schools. They are helped, at school, to open their minds to science and to the marvels of creation. But in how many of these boys and girls, at the end of their schooling, is to be found the desire and, more still, the *anxiety* to discover the face of God – 'the thirst of him who is their Creator', in the words of the saintly Bishop of Hippo. We have to admit, in all humility, that if that does not happen, if in our Christian educational establishments the children only receive 'knowledge' but not the 'wisdom' they need for life, then we have failed in our task.

Another great Father of the Church, St Ignatius of Antioch, has given us in a nutshell what the essential requirements of any educational endeavour should be: 'One educates a lot by what one says,' he writes, 'and still more by what one does, and more still by what one is.'

It is right to try to discover methods of education that are more apt to meet the needs of the times in which we live. It is necessary to pay great attention to 'all that is said' in our schools, to the didactic techniques that are employed; and likewise 'to all that is done' in them, the concrete initiatives that are taken so that the school fulfils its purpose. But it is equally necessary, if not more so, to realise that, for all those who are engaged in the school, the lasting fruit of the education that is given is derived above all from 'what one is'. I believe that we all carry with us the proof of that affirmation: we remember with gratitude the figure of one or other of the teachers we have known; we are grateful for what they have given us through the example of their lives even more than through the words or the subject matter of their teaching.

The Church is deeply aware of this requirement; she knows she must teach by virtue of what she is, according to the wishes of her founder, that is to say, a 'community of faith, hope and charity, a visible organisation through which he communicates truth and grace to all men' (LG, n. 8). The Church fulfils her mission by living the command she has received from Christ: 'Go out to the whole world; proclaim the Gospel to all creation' (Mk 16:16). This is the concrete way in which the Church is called upon to continue in time that 'power of healing' that emanated from Jesus and drew the crowds to him, as St Mark tells us in today's Gospel.

All the effort we make to keep our educational establishments alive is only meaningful if it is lived as a concrete fulfilment of the command of evangelisation received from Jesus. It is only of significance if all we do opens up a path that leads to him. The essence of the evangelical message is *Christ* – and not so much his doctrine as his person. Education is meaningful for the Church if it is carried out as a form of evangelisation; but evangelisation can only be 'a path to friendship with Christ'.

If we are not just content to 'pass on notions' but truly wish to help the children 'to grow in wisdom', then we must help them above all to have a grasp of *true* life by showing them the way that leads to its fulfilment: 'Lord we do not know where you are going, so how can we know the way?' (Jn 14:1-9). Thomas's words still ring today in a world where so many ways are proposed to young people to lead them to the full realisation of their lives. We must have the courage to propose the way that Jesus himself pointed out: 'I am the way, the truth and the life … whoever comes to me will see the Father' (Ibid.). Jesus is the way in so far as he is the truth and reveals God's nature to us; he is the way in so far as he is the life, the fullness of being and the utmost expression of authentic existence.

At this point we must be courageous and ask ourselves the unavoidable question: What do they know of Christ, as a person, those boys and girls at the end of their term of study in our schools? What is the lasting idea, the life-long image they have of Christ by having gone through our schools?

It is now time for us to enter together into the mystery of the Eucharist that places us at the very heart of the person of Christ and also at the heart of our social responsibilities. The children and young people entrusted to our care expect very much of the Church, and perhaps more than they themselves are willing to admit. They do not expect us to teach them what they can simply learn from others or perhaps in a different manner, but rather what we alone can teach them, because to us has been given the deposit of the faith and the mission of handing it on in the name of Christ.

The Church was born of the Eucharist when Christ asked his disciples to perpetuate in time his supreme gesture of love, the total self-giving that is anticipated in the mystery of his words: 'Do this in memory of me.' This is the source of the Church's authority to proclaim the message that has been given her by her founder; it is from here that she derives the authority to teach and educate.

To preside, to be seated in a chair of learning, is to bear responsibility. The person who teaches presides, but must above all preside with charity, with love. And to preside with charity means being anchored in the Eucharist, which is the real presence of love incarnate, the Body and Blood offered up for us.

A few days ago, in the message sent to the plenary meeting of the Congregation for Catholic Education, the Holy Father said: 'In the context of globalisation and the mutual interaction of peoples and cultures, the Church feels the pressing need to preach the Gospel and wishes to live it with renewed missionary zeal. Catholic education appears to be, therefore, more and more the fruit of a mission that must be "shared" by priests, consecrated persons and the lay faithful.'

May our participation in this Eucharist help us to understand a little better the meaning of the mission that has been entrusted to us and renew our commitment to live it intensely, not simply because it is part of a long and glorious tradition in our country, but because we value it as a precious heritage to be lived with renewed generosity and enlightened courage, seeking to find new approaches and better methods of proposing the perennial message given us by Jesus our Master in our changed historical circumstances.

And may we be accompanied by the motherly intercession of Mary, *Sedes Sapientiae*, to whose work of education we owe

the marvellous humanity of Christ, the instrument by which he
brought about our salvation.

Issues in Catholic Education in Ireland

David Tuohy

INTRODUCTION

In considering issues related to Catholic schools and their future, it is important to acknowledge a number of contested areas. The first is the understanding of Catholic. The second is the purpose of schooling. This naturally leads to a third area, where attempts are made to integrate the two areas in a Catholic school.

CATHOLIC

In 1974, Avery Dulles wrote a book entitled *Models of the Church*. In it he explored different analogies, or models, to describe the Church, mindful that in order to do justice to the complex reality of the Church, different models must be held simultaneously. Four of these models are presented here as relevant to our review of the Church's involvement in education in Ireland: Church as Institution, the Church as Communion and the models of Herald and Sacrament are considered together.

Church as Institution
The *Church as Institution* has been a common model since the late middle ages. In this model, the Church is seen as a society, with visible structures, functions and powers. In general, the functions

and powers are defined as teaching, sanctifying and governing. This gives rise to structures which distinguish between the Church teaching and the Church taught; the Church sanctifying and the Church sanctified; and the Church governing and the Church governed. The Church that teaches, sanctifies and governs is identified with the hierarchical governing body. The marks of this model of Church are clericalist, juridicist and triumphalistic. Membership is clearly defined as those who are baptised and who profess the doctrines, communicate in the sacraments and submit themselves in obedience to the legitimate pastors.

Church as Communion
This model of Church builds on the biblical images of the *Body of Christ* and the *People of God*. It focuses on the intimacy shared in primary groups. These groups are based on fellowship – the fellowship of humankind with God (the vertical dimension) and with one another in Christ (the horizontal dimension). Membership is no longer a juridical term, but rather a mystical or spiritual concept depicting the relationship between all who have been touched by the Spirit of God. The Church, from this perspective, is a communion of people. The bonds are primarily the interior graces of the Holy Spirit – faith, hope and charity – but these are also expressed by external bonds of creed, worship and ecclesiastical fellowship. The intimacy of the horizontal dimension also promotes solidarity and sharing among the members. The Church is both the expression of this fellowship as well as being the means by which the fellowship is produced and maintained. In *Lumen gentium*, Vatican II's document on the church, the term 'People of God' was used in very broad terms and was not confined to the Catholic Church.

Church as Herald and Sacrament
The *Church as Herald* sees the Church as gathered and formed by the word of God. It exists in any congregation where the word is

proclaimed and faithfully heard. Its mission is to proclaim that which it has heard and believed. The emphasis is on faith and proclamation over relationships and communion. All else is secondary to proclaiming the word with integrity and persistence. In effect, this theology rejects a theology of glory, where the word of God is seen as already present in some way within the Church. It insists on the continual need for conversion, both in hearing (where the focus is *within*) and proclaiming (where the focus is *external*). Closely linked with this model is the model of *Church as Sacrament*. As such, it is a sign and instrument of the intimate union of God with humankind. It is the historically tangible form of the redeeming grace of Christ. This sign has an outer dimension – the structure of the church – and an inner dimension – the life of faith, hope and love that makes the church a dynamic presence in culture. The *Church as Herald* is a direct approach to preaching the word. The *Church as Sacrament* is more indirect, as it depends on the ability of the observer to interpret the sign. In both models, the Church is called to self-reform, in developing integrity in preaching the Word and in becoming an authentic sign.

The institutional model of Church can be seen in the identification of religion with attendance at mass and the sacraments. It has its consequence in the emphasis on the administrative role of parish clergy, and the concern for the future of parishes with the decline in clerical numbers. On the moral front there has been a greater rejection of the teaching authority of the institutional Church, especially in sexual ethics. The community model of Church is evident in the more casual affiliation of people with the institution, yet proclaiming a Catholic identity. People who work from this model focus on spirituality rather than on religion. They attend mass at Christmas and Easter, and use church services for baptism, marriages and funerals. This model is also evident in the growth of primary groups of committed church-goers for bible study, discussion and mutual support. Similarly, many people engaged in voluntary parish ministry, such as members of choir and ministers of the Eucharist, appreciate the fellowship of their peers as much as the content of their activity. The evangelist model can be observed in the growth of the RCIA programme, in the work of retreats and missions at parish and diocesan level and in the witness given by the presence of religious and lay volunteer groups in marginalised communities.

The different models of Church can be experienced partly as a reality of the Catholic Church in Ireland today and partly as the frustrated aspiration of those who want to be called Catholic and play an active role in their church. The emphasis on new models of affiliation to the Church is reflected in other areas of culture as well – work, marriage and politics. The tensions experienced within the Church reflect the human dimension of a church that is deeply affected by the very culture it tries to influence.

Models of Church in Educational Provision

Church involvement in education in Ireland developed from a highly institutional model. Emerging at the time of Catholic Emancipation, the battle to establish schools for Catholics was a sign of a growing confidence in a previously suppressed Church. The history of that period shows strong sectarian politics, where the bishops played a strong leadership role in asserting the right of Catholics to establish separate schools. Undoubtedly part of the aim was to establish the Church as a highly visible presence in the country. The education goals included the development of Catholic lay people who would play an active part in the politics and culture of the country, guided in their values and decision making by the Church teaching. The ultimate aim was the establishment of a Catholic state. This period also gave rise to the establishment of a number of strong native congregations (Christian Brothers, Mercy and Presentation Sisters).

As a result, the Church and nationalist politics made easy bedfellows. Irish spirituality was a mixture of piety and national fervour. There was a strong link between being Irish and being Catholic. In education, this approach was seen in the school curriculum and in school organisation. As well as a strong emphasis on the traditional 3 R's, there was an inclusion of a stylised version of Irish history and an emphasis on Irish culture in language, music and dance. Religious congregations set up their monastery and convent schools, and the national school system developed through the patronage of the diocesan bishops, with the local parish clergy playing a major managerial role. Diocesan advisors and examiners were appointed whose sole remit was with the quality of religious instruction. This approach contrasts with other jurisdictions such as Australia and New Zealand, where the Catholic Education Office has a whole school remit, and has a different relationship with the government inspectorate.

A feature of post-primary education provision was the influx of international congregations to work in Ireland, and the low level of diocesan involvement other than through the affiliation of different congregations to local bishops and the minor seminaries. Post-primary education was for the elite. There was a strong emphasis on a classical education, with no attention to vocational education – although parish clergy were appointed to many VEC boards and worked in these schools. In the early years of the state, there was an identification of the school with Irish culture. Many schools taught through the medium of Irish (although this may have reflected more the need for extra funding than a commitment to the language itself). Religious knowledge consisted mainly of the catechism and apologetics, and reinforced the traditional piety of the home. External monitoring took place through the bishop's examination. Little attention was paid to the study of the Bible – in fact, reading the Bible was something Protestants did. For Catholics, the word of God was mediated at Mass. They experienced the sacraments *ex opere operato* (by virtue of the ritual) rather than *ex opere operantis* (by virtue of their disposition). At an organisational level, there was a strong emphasis on discipline, and this was often reinforced with punishment. The teachers were mainly clerics and religious, and the lay teachers were regarded as helpers.

In effect, the institutional Church provided an education *for Catholics*. D'Arbon has described this as a time when Catholic cows ate Catholic grass in Catholic fields. There was a strong sense of identity in the membership of the schools, and students were fed a strong diet of Catholic orthodoxy with the aim of strengthening the Church. However, it is far less easy to identify Catholic cows nowadays, or fields where they eat. Also, their diet is more from the *á la carte* menu.

Vatican II brought a major shift in the way the Church thought about itself. The effects of the Council on the internal dynamics of the Church were contemporaneous with major developments in education in Ireland. At primary level there was a new curriculum that was more child-centred than the previous content-centred approach. Corporal punishment was also abolished. This gave rise to relationships in the classroom, focusing on the pupil's affiliation to school through positive intrinsic motivation rather than through extrinsic factors or fear.

The introduction of free education at post-primary level gave rise to a major influx of new students. This also created an expansion of the teaching force well beyond the resources of the religious congregations. In fact, the religious congregations were in some internal turmoil in facing the challenges of Vatican II. Many members left the congregations to embrace a more positive theology of work and marriage (Breen). Within congregations, the demand to return to the founding charism gave rise to questions about traditional institutional works. Many congregations changed direction, opting for work at community level in solidarity with marginalised groups in society. This fitted easily with the new community-building orientation of the Church.

Schools were also challenged to develop a community orientation. Many of the new student cohort in Irish schools came from backgrounds that had no experience of post-primary education, yet they aspired more to the secondary rather than the vocational sector. This meant that secondary schools were meeting a very different calibre of student, one which they had traditionally avoided in the dual academic/vocational arrangement. High failure rates soon made it apparent that the traditional academic education on offer was not helpful, and so began a series of curricular initiatives to link more with student experiences and needs. Allied with this, schools developed pastoral care initiatives to help students. Religious education also changed. In the wake of the doubts cast on the institutional certainties of the past, new approaches to catechesis developed which saw a greater emphasis on discussion of moral issues rather than on formal doctrine.

At an organisational level, the traditional institutional, hierarchical model was very strong. The congregations saw the schools as their 'family firm', and they exercised ownership and control rights. They held on to positions of power as principals and later as chairpersons of Boards of Management. The expansion of the second-level system, allied with the lack of vocations, has meant that religious are a rapidly declining percentage of the teaching force. They found it increasingly difficult to find high-calibre individuals among their members to fill key positions. There was also a dispute with the second-level teachers' trade union over the rights and roles of lay teachers in religious-run schools. This gave rise to quite complex systems of in-school management and decision making. Within the Church, congregations were developing new insights into collaborative ministry. At the same time, the political system was promoting a rhetoric on partnership. In education, there was widespread consultation on the future of education. Also, partnership models of governance through Boards of Management emerged as a norm. These factors contributed to a major shift in thinking about the role of religious in schools.

As well as developments at post-primary level, there was also a major expansion of the education system to include adult learning. The rhetoric shifted from the formal schooling process to that of life-long learning. This had particular impact on second-chance learning for those who missed out on earlier opportunities. Some of these developments have been at an informal level, and many individual religious have contributed to this area. On a formal level, the country has seen a growth in training agencies, and also the proliferation of many community support groups running parallel to the formal schooling system. These groups focus on parenting skills, personal development for adults, as well as aiming for formal qualifications.

The period of economic expansion since the late 1960s has had an overall positive effect on the Irish economy. Over the past ten years that growth has been spectacular, a phenomenon known as the Celtic Tiger. As well as contributing to an increased standard of living, there has been a major shift in cultural values. For many commentators, Ireland is well on the way to being a post-Christian society with an increase in secularism and materialism (Cassidy, Gallagher). This is not unique to Ireland and reflects the globalisation of value systems. In more recent years, the country has seen the erosion of traditional values from within its own culture. It now also has to face the integration of new cultures due to an increasing international profile in its own population. This changed culture has posed new problems for Catholic schools. In the community model of the Church, there was an assumption that people believed and shared values, even if they did not always accede to the institutional demands. Now, however, many Catholic schools find that the students do not know the rudiments of the Christian story. Far from being a community based on Catholic values, schools find themselves introducing pupils to these values, sometimes with little or no home support. Catholic identity in this situation is that of the Church as Evangelist. Catholic schools have changed their focus from an education for Catholics to a *Catholic education for all.* There is a search for the value dimension of the school that both proclaims the word of God and witnesses to it in a way that engages in a dynamic dialogue between faith and culture. It must also be said that this dialogue impacts as much on some of the teachers as it does on the students and their families.

Challenges for Catholic Identity

As I stated at the outset, the understanding of Catholic is a contested area. It is contested in the internal forum, as we try to define an identity that is faithful to our past and yet integrate different insights from psychology, science, sociology and theology. The Church struggles to respond to the challenges posed by a very different life experience of its members. It also struggles to learn from its own sinfulness and what, with hindsight, has been an abuse of power. Catholic is also contested in the external forum, where the right of the Church to manage publicly funded schools in a pluralist society is more frequently disputed.

How can these challenges be conceived as they impact on our understanding of Church, particularly the model of Church we bring to the ministry of education? I would like to focus on four such challenges in particular.

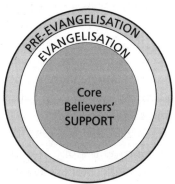

Figure 1. *A model of the response of schools to various levels of engagement with religious belief*

28

Firstly, there is a need to explore the model of Church that best fits the age and culture we work in. It seems to me that the Church deals with three levels of Christian participation (Figure 1). The first is a form of pre-evangelisation, which develops the human capacity of the individual. The second level is evangelisation, where that human capacity is named as participation in the life of God. In education the school witnesses, by word and sacrament in the more general sense, to the presence of God in the community. It seeks to introduce students to the story and person of Jesus so that they can see their human potential fulfilled in him. A third level is one of support, which provides nourishment to those who are committed to their faith. This is done through rituals, teaching and prayerful reflection on experience.

These three levels of participation exist simultaneously in any community, and to a certain extent always have. Yet, the balance of activities that respond to the needs of the community has changed. There is now a greater need for attention to pre-evangelisation and evangelisation than there was forty years ago. If we continue to act out of models of support in the types of ritual we employ, then we are likely to do a serious injustice to both the people we serve and the message of the Gospel. I believe this is true for pastoral strategy at diocesan and parish level, as well as at school level.

A second challenge is related to the theological language we use. The theology of my youth can be classified as a redemptive theology. There was a sense that God had made a perfect world in the Garden, and that we had somehow messed it up, and continued to do so. Our lives were about seeking redemption, and making reparation for that sinfulness. In many ways, we were more conscious of sin than of love. A different approach is to take the second story of the Garden, and to see God inviting us to work with him to build up creation. The approach here is creationist: it takes seriously the implications of Jesus working his miracles on the Sabbath; the creator is no longer resting, but is continually at work building up creation. The two approaches are radically different, and need to be explored. Certainly, young people empathise more with a theology of creation and are alienated by the strong emphasis on redemption they hear in church. It leads them to associate religion with something for older people, rather than for them (Tuohy and Cairns). Creation is a language of growth and development; redemption is a language of preservation and reclamation. The experience of learning, especially in the modern curriculum, is also one of creation. The process of evangelisation in schools needs to find some congruence with the learning process which is the main business of the school.

A third challenge is to see faith development as a partnership between home, school and parish. We talk of the Catholic school, but the school is inserted into a local community. If the school sees itself as the Church, and provides the only experience of religious community for young people, then it will be very difficult to manage the transition between the world of school and the world of adulthood. Religion will become part of the nostalgia associated with 'the best days of their life'. There is a need for strong alliances between schools and the local church, at parish and diocesan level, in supporting young people. Similarly, this cannot happen without the support of the home. There needs to be mutual support for the value systems being taught and for the ways of teaching them. As approaches to religious education changed, many parents were left confused. Those who were keen to help did not understand these new approaches and, in general, little effort was made to inform them. Parents also need nourishment. Not only do they need to develop their own adult spirituality, they need encouragement in their role of passing on the faith. Being an adult does not necessarily prepare you for Christian parenting.

A fourth challenge is to examine the baggage we carry because of our own sense of the institutional Church. I will return to this later in the paper, but it is important to state at the outset that we have been formed by our own experience of church. There is a danger that when we come to systematise some of the new insights we have learnt, we will try to package them in structures with which we are familiar, rather than seeking new structures for a new way of thinking. In particular, we must examine our own tendency to reproduce hierarchical models of governance under the guise that at least we are much more benign than previous generations.

SCHOOL

As we have seen, Catholic is a contested concept. So too is the concept of school. Let me make an important distinction here between education and school. They are not synonymous. Education is the grand term for worthwhile learning, no matter where it takes place or its source. Schooling, by contrast, is the way a society invests in particular experiences for its citizens. As such, it is a political concept and open to change as the needs of a society changes.

I would like to highlight a number of key tensions in the provision of schooling. These are by no means exhaustive. Like the models of Church, the different tensions exist at the same time, like a juggler keeping many balls in the air.

Schools as Organisation

Our schools hold a tension between the charisma attached to individual teachers and the idea of a streamlined, cohesive organisation focused on measurable goals. Our schools emerged from a largely agrarian model – the hedge schools in Ireland or the small country schoolhouse. Much depended on the individual teacher. The organisation of the school year, with the long summer holidays, reflects the rhythms of farming life much more than life in the city. It was only with the industrial revolution that the movement to mass education came about, and here the organisation of schools took on a more industrial approach – according to some commentators, in order to prepare young people for the drudgery of the production line. Indeed, the organisation of post-primary schools into forty minute slots, with the regular ringing of bells, has little to do with the optimum approach to learning. It has much to do with the efficient delivery of a complex curriculum and the orderly movement of people. The drive for uniformity and predictability in school organisation has continued, driven mainly by the need for accountability and transparency in the use of public funds (Sarason). As with many other organisations, there is now a greater demand for legal compliance to government rules and regulations. These regulations in part protect individuals in the workplace and in part protect the investment of funding.

Schools and Knowledge
There has always been a tension in schools with the idea of learning – whether knowledge was seen in the content that students acquired, or whether more emphasis was placed on the process of learning. The demands of completing a curriculum often force teachers to take short cuts on the process in order to cover the content. There are times when we would like to wait for that 'eureka' moment in the classroom, but move on because of pressure of time. We have an idealism of what knowledge will do for the individual – making them wise and holistic individuals – yet we are constrained by the need to acquire information in order to reproduce it in exams. At times, we spend our time collecting the wood, but have little appreciation of the trees from which that wood comes.

With the complexity of modern life and the increasing demands on schools, it is easy to be lured into a view of knowledge as mere information and to forget its transformative impact on individuals. Knowledge gives power and freedom, but it can also be treated as a commodity. Curriculum development in Ireland over the past twenty years or so has shown a high level of commitment to the process of learning and active methodologies. Unfortunately, this has not translated into a reform of the examination system or the culture related to these exams. Our modern culture sees knowledge as something to be acquired. Achievement is demonstrated through amassing credentials, and many commentators have remarked that education credentials are replacing land as a means to power and position (Lynch, Clancy et al.). This can give rise to a utilitarian approach to learning, which has a major influence on the culture of schools and classrooms. In particular, with the growth of third-level education as a norm for high-level employment, post-primary and primary education are increasingly means to an end – entry to third level – rather than ends in themselves – the formation of holistic individuals, which is the aim of many of our mission statements.

Schools and Achievement
Closely linked to the tension around knowledge is a tension on how we look at achievement. Achievement can be seen as a criterion-referenced event – we define a skill or a task to be completed and the student strives for that standard. The reference for success is in relation to the criterion set in the task. Achievement can also be measured in norm-referenced ways, where success is judged not in reference to the task, but in reference to other people. You are measured on how well you do compared with others, or on the number of skills you acquire or tasks you complete relative to your peers. The Irish system has been very good in promoting the idea of individual education plans for pupils with special needs, but this has not extended to mainstream education yet.

In primary schools, the culture of learning tends to be more criterion referenced, although there is always a pressure to keep pupils moving up with their peers based on chronological age. This means that many pass from one class to the next without mastering some basic skills. As the gap between their current knowledge and the demands of the curriculum grows, they experience problems with achievement and self-esteem, and they need remedial attention. In post-primary schools, the approach is more norm referenced. This sets up cultures of competition rather than cooperation. The examination system at post-primary level in Ireland is based on norm-referenced assessment. This gives rise to cultures in classrooms of summative rather than formative assessment. The effects of this approach can be seen in the way students value themselves in relation to their learning and the number of points they achieve in their Leaving Certificate.

Although widespread, this competitive culture is held in tension. We still hear teachers proclaim that they get as much, if not more, satisfaction when a weak student passes, or gets a C, as when the high flyer gets an A1 on the higher paper. This reflects a criterion-referenced approach. However, teachers also get trapped into evaluating their own competence through student results. They are caught in the culture of league tables that confuse successful learning with successful performance in examinations, and rate schools on only one part of their mission to students – academic achievement – rather than holistic personal development, a norm-referenced approach.

Schools and the Economy

Linked with the notion of achievement is the role of schools in the economy. Parents and students have an expectation that schools will prepare young people for the world of work. However, they can do that in two ways. One is to focus on the individual and help them explore their talents and commit to developing these talents for themselves and in the service of others. The second approach is to focus on the system, where schools sort out the talent according to predetermined skills to make for easy identification of the human capital available to the economy.

There has been much debate in recent years on the contribution of education to economic growth. There is a clear rhetoric that an investment in education pays off for the individual in terms of employability. There is also a greater demand on education to supply the economy with particular core skills. The tension here can be characterised as a tension between a focus on a *standard of living* (where the focus is on earning power, production, competition, GDP) and *a quality of life* (where the focus is on happiness, satisfactory relationships, lifestyle). There is no doubt that our standard of living has increased, but we can also question whether the quality of life we must live in order to maintain that standard is an improvement. Schools hold this tension in their approach to career guidance in the way they value achievement and ambition in their students, and in their ability to integrate humanistic values into these areas.

Schools and Values

Schools are commissioned to transmit the values of a society to the young. There are many different approaches to values. We can characterise the tension that exists as a polarity between an intrinsic and an extrinsic dynamic. The intrinsic dynamic is built around a community approach. By helping young people to live in community, they learn respect and tolerance of others. They also learn about the relationship between their own needs and that of the common good. They learn that the common good is determined not just by numbers but by the authenticity of the values that are embraced. By learning in this way, it is hoped that the young people come to internalise the values they explore. The extrinsic approach demands compliance to an *a priori* set of values. These values are the outcome of well-tried experience in the community and reflect a traditional approach to work and to dealing with others, especially those in authority.

The tension over values transmission can be seen in the way teachers talk about discipline in schools and the growing problem in some places with a highly disaffected youth. I remember working in one school which had a highly streamed system. One teacher described the school: 'To the top stream we give an education – there are lots of opportunities for personal growth and new experiences. To the middle stream, we give teaching – we focus on getting them through the exams and performing well, in fact, helping them to overachieve. The bottom stream, well, we give them discipline – we try to control them, not to have too many expectations and not to let them disrupt the rest of the school.' You can imagine how that approach might have reinforced certain types of behaviour in the students.

School Policies
Discipline, as discussed above, is a key school policy and many trustees have taken an active role in the development of these policies. There are other areas as well where tensions exist in schools. One such area is in the question of admissions. Particularly in post-primary schools, where schools are meeting a more disengaged youth population, there is often nostalgia for the good old days 'when nice, well-behaved children attended this school'. Part of the demand on principals is to cut off the problem at the pass – by refusing admission to potential problems. But this is impossible, both for legal and economic reasons. Many trustees have made it a point that admission to their schools is non-selective and government policy insists on open admissions, including the mainstreaming of special needs students. Yet one often hears teachers reflect on the need to balance the number of 'these types of students' in the school, and the effect of taking such pupils on the intake of 'high flyers', often upper-middle-class students. This tension is not just teachers seeking a comfort zone. It can exhibit a real concern for the individual student. It is indeed questionable whether keeping a highly disaffected student in school says more about the system's need for numbers and order than it does about

concern for the individual's need. There are growing opportunities for alternative learning pathways. Some of these exist in the various schemes between the Department of Education and Science and the Department of Enterprise, Trade and Employment. Others are tailored to different stages of adult development, as part of a strategy of lifelong learning.

The growth of different types of exclusive schools in the country indicates that some parents are prepared to invest heavily in preserving a social elitism for their children. The involvement of Church groups in these schools remains a point of controversy and debate. In general, however, the Catholic school proclaims a policy of taking all pupils. This is often a countercultural witness that gives dignity to each individual. However, we must be clear of the implications of such a policy. Schools can *accept* all pupils, but they may not *welcome* them all in the same way. Policies of inclusion are not just related to admission but also involve the way students are organised in streamed classes within the school. As outlined above in the section on values, such policies can radically affect the quality of a child's experience of the school.

Challenges for the Future

When considering the tensions that schools face, the task confronting Trustees, Boards of Management and school leadership into the future is extremely challenging. It seems to me that the challenge can be summarised in the need to balance three perspectives on education – meaning, community and excellence. Within each of these perspectives there are challenges to leadership in developing the future as well as in servicing the present (Figure 2).

Figure 2. *Three goals of school leadership and the tasks associated with these goals*

'Meaning' refers to developing a common vision about what the school is trying to achieve, balancing personal, spiritual, career and economic goals. 'Community' refers to how the people in the school can work together and the relationships that develop between them. 'Excellence' refers to standards in personal, academic, behavioural and extra-curricular achievements.

There are powerful forces at work in seeking to control education. Many of these do not share either the view of the human person so central to Catholic education or a philosophy of how schools enter into a dialogue with culture and help students to a critical appreciation of that culture. It seems to me to be of critical importance that there be a clear philosophy of education that we can espouse and support – if not for the whole country, at least as an option within it. Looking at the development of these tensions in Ireland, it is perhaps noticeable that the voice of the Catholic trustees has been somewhat muted. However, individual members of congregations have played a major role in curriculum development at national level. CORI published a number of prophetic and well researched documents on disadvantage in education in the 1990s, and individual schools have taken creative approaches to programme development, particularly in Transition Year. Yet the schools remain remarkably dependent on curricular initiatives from the Department of Education and Science. There is a paralysis that any personal initiative may well disadvantage students in the examination system. There seems to be a fear that helping students to be better people is not productive. However, my evidence for this is more anecdotal than substantively based. Yet, I know for a fact that many trustees have not engaged with their schools – their teachers and the parents – in discussing these issues. They have been more concerned with the maintenance function of schooling than in taking a leadership role in education. They have developed a strong sense of community in schools, with stress on pastoral care. Many have invested in supporting the RE programme and RE teachers as a discrete unit. In general, however, they have not engaged with staff in a discussion of the philosophy of the overall curriculum and the contribution of individual subjects to the overall aim.

The education arena has become much more complex in recent years. This complexity poses problems for governance that are radically different from the types of issues faced by previous generations of religious in schools. It is vital that, in planning for the future, we do not try to put new wine into old skins. Developing systems and structures which demand that future generations of lay people are compliant to a prescribed ethos is really an attempt to capture a nostalgic view of the past. It does scant justice to the complexity and dynamism of the development of schools, or to the changed context of evangelisation. Any view that sees the resolution of the tensions outlined above as something that can be prescribed in advance, as a product, is not facing reality. From the perspective of the old cartoon, we are nomads on a journey; we are not people of the oasis, settling down to a certain and predictable future.

In considering the future of Catholic education, we must realise that Catholic schools will be the same as all other schools, no other schools and some other schools, all at the same time. We will share many concerns with schools involved purely in a humanistic approach to education. A challenge is to see what the term 'Catholic' adds to the school. One way to look at this is to examine the role of faith formation in the dynamic of education. There are two approaches. One is to see the 'Catholic' dimension as an added extra to the school – a kind of icing on the cake. The school runs its own powerful dynamic, but also incorporates rituals that reflect Catholic values. They are almost an optional extra, in that those who do not like the icing can leave it on the side. The second approach is to see the Catholic dimension as the leaven. It is a pervasive presence in the school, informing all aspects of the school. At curricular level, it is not just the preserve of the Religious Education programme; it is something that informs all subjects. There may not be a Catholic mathematics, but there may well be a Catholic way of teaching and learning the subject. The tension outlined here gives rise to a consideration of the integration of the notion of Catholic and school.

INTEGRATION

Model of Church

Model of School	Institution	Communion	Herald/ Sacrament
Organisation			
Knowledge			
Achievement			
Economy			
Values			
Policies			

Figure 3. *A framework for conceptualising the integration of Church and school*

The integration of Catholic perspectives and educational perspectives is a key element for the Catholic school. Schools are described in Vatican documents as centres of evangelisation. They also have a powerful dynamic of their own, situated in the social, cultural and political climate of Ireland in the twenty-first century. The tensions that exist in schooling can be resolved in many different ways and the solutions will be congruent with some models of Church, and may be in conflict with others (Figure 3). An interesting exercise is to take different aspects of a school and describe how they reflect different perspectives of the Church. If completed honestly, an examination of the columns and the lines of a grid such as that shown above can reveal much about the Catholic identity of a school. In some ways, schools can domesticate a particular perspective of the Church within their own dynamic. Similarly, different perspectives on the Church's mission can inform an approach to schooling. The challenge is to find the most appropriate model for our age, a model that is faithful to the message of the Gospel and to the mandate to 'Go forth, and teach all nations', and to do so in a language that is understood. In facing this future, I would like to dwell on two major challenges – governance structures and leadership succession.

Governance Structures
As outlined above, we inherit models of governance that are hierarchical and bureaucratic. This is true in Church and in political arenas. There is a great danger that we will continue these structures into the future, with a set of impossible demands on those who take up office. Already we see the reluctance of many good people to take on leadership roles in education. It is difficult to get them to sit on Boards of Management and it is difficult to get good teachers to apply for the role of principal.

As we look to the future, our structures must allow and support creative development. Our goal cannot be to enshrine

41

the past by copper-fastening the notion of ethos and putting in place systems of monitoring and accountability that place impossible burdens on future generations – burdens that we ourselves did not embrace or live up to in the past. Neither can we demand a particular type of response to a new and complex reality, when we ourselves will not be involved in that future. The ethos of Catholic schools is not an easily defined product or identity. To think so is to make the Holy Spirit redundant and to deny his or her continual activity in history. It is to deny the incarnation in culture as being the unique understanding of how the Christian God relates to humankind. Our structures for governance must embody and support the dynamic element of discernment. As we look to the future, we are not writing our wills in order to leave our wealth to others. It is not ours to give. Instead, we are rewriting and reinterpreting a covenant. This covenant points us back to Gospel values rather than congregational ownership. Our inspiration comes from the history of God's dealing with humankind and the teaching of Jesus. Congregations and their founders are particular embodiments of that teaching. We should not confuse the sign and that to which the sign points.

In discerning this future, congregations face a real challenge. Trustees have a legal responsibility with regard to property and ownership; yet, at a moral level, they are only stewards of the schooling enterprise. Much of the property they 'own' has been donated to them by generous benefactors. It has been maintained by government grants for capital and current expenditure, by responses to fundraising appeals as well as the generous and self-sacrificing service of many religious over the years – especially in the early days of the state when there was very little support for education. We cannot let the paternalism of our approach in the past cloud the fact that the development of education in Ireland has been a community affair, and we need to acknowledge that in the future structures of governance.

Leadership Succession

A second concern for the future arises when we look for those who will continue the work of governing Catholic schools. The image that members of religious congregations will provide that leadership from their zimmerframes is inappropriate. We are looking to a largely lay future. However, we have done very little to provide for, or to develop a capacity among our lay colleagues for that future. In general, we have been blessed by the first generation of lay principals, those who have taught alongside religious and imbibed by osmosis the value systems. However, the pace of change in Irish education has been so fast that the second generation of lay principals will have little experience of religious as educators. Their knowledge of Catholic education will be second hand. And in general, our laity has not been nourished on a theological level, particularly in a theology that reflects on professional experience in education. To a large extent, the institutional model of the past has given theological in-service to the clergy and members of religious congregations, and left a theologically illiterate laity. Lay principals comment regularly that their religious formation finished at the end of secondary school and they feel very inadequate in leading the spiritual dimension of the school.

Thankfully, there are major changes in the provision for a lay theology, but as of yet this has not impacted on educational leadership to any great extent. It is true that many trustees provide opportunities for principals and Boards of Management to reflect on Gospel issues. However, this approach depends on getting good people into position first, then giving them in-service. There is an urgent need to expand that approach to develop capacity within the system. Those who may apply for leadership positions need to be introduced to key concepts much earlier in their careers. They need to be given a fluency in theological language and reflection. However, this is not just something for schools. It will be impossible to ask lay people to lead the future of Catholic education when we give them no role in the church where they can develop these skills.

Developing this capacity will be a challenge. We must also remember that many teachers teaching in Catholic schools are not necessarily committed to Catholic education as a value. They are there because they are committed to teaching as a career, and, in Ireland, the only schools available to them are Catholic ones. Their commitment to the Catholic dimension of the school depends on, and may be limited to, areas where there is common ground between expressed Catholic values and sound educational approaches. This is a major challenge to the validity of a specifically Catholic dimension to our schools.

Imagery is important in understanding this challenge. Leadership studies in recent years have seen a return to the idea of biography. This has been inspired by a renewed interest in archetypes as a way of describing different approaches to leadership functions. In scripture, there are three main archetypes of leadership:

- **The King** in the history of Israel was responsible for bringing peace to the people by guarding it against external enemies and by promoting justice within the kingdom.
- **The Priest** was charged with keeping the people in touch with the meaning of their calling through reading and interpreting the books of the law, and through ritual.

Both these ministries in Israel were inherited ministries – they were passed down in different tribes.

- **The Prophet**, on the other hand, was specially called by God to confront the king, the priest and the people, and to remind them of their relationship to the covenant and to call them to repentance.

It is an interesting reflection to see how these roles can be applied in educational leadership. The royal role in managing the school against external forces and dispensing justice within the school is fairly obvious. The priestly role of helping people to get in touch with the vision of education and the truth of their relationship with God can also be seen in many areas of school leadership. The role of prophet is less obvious, but there is need for a critical reflection on the direction of education, and particularly the direction of our own schools. It is important that we grasp this role as well as the other two.

Each of us, as Christians, shares in these roles. We are not given these roles because we are appointed to positions of authority within the church or within a school. We have not been given these gifts in more abundance because we are clerics or members of a religious congregation. We share them through our baptism. It is important that we recognise these gifts in the entirety of the Christian community. We cannot reserve the prophetic function to ourselves and delegate the royal and priestly functions elsewhere. There must be a holism in our partnership with others. Our stewardship of schools follows another great archetype from scripture – the servant leader, proclaimed by Jesus. However, the service we offer is not that of slaves, but of healing and reconciliation.

Undoubtedly, at this time, we will be tempted to different types of stewardship, just as Jesus was tempted in the desert to become a different type of Messiah. There would be advantages in having control over things and resources; to have status and respect, and to have power and ownership over many kingdoms and schools. However, we must see that for what it is – a temptation. There is a need to discern the proper role in governance together. I see this time as a time when we walk, like the two disciples on the road to Emmaus, low in morale, down-hearted and deep in discussion about recent events. My hope is that this current dialogue will help explain the scriptures to us again, so that our hearts burn within us, leading us forward with new vision and new energy.

REFERENCES

Breen, M.J. (ed.) *A Fire in the Forest*, Dublin: Veritas, 2001.

Cassidy, E., *Faith and Culture in the Irish Context*, Dublin: Veritas, 1996.
Measuring Ireland: Discerning Values and Beliefs, Dublin: Veritas, 2002.

Clancy, P., Drudy, S., Lynch, K. and O'Dowd, L. (eds) *Irish Society: Sociological Perspectives*, Dublin: IPA, 1995, especially Part 3.

D'Arbon, T., 'Stimulus Paper 3' in Duignan, P. and D'Arbon, T. (eds) *Conversations in Cyber-Space: Challenges and Paradoxes for Catholic Leaders*, Australian Catholic University, 1998.

Dulles, A., *Models of the Church*, Dublin: Gill & Macmillan, 1977.

Gallagher, M.P., *Clashing Symbols: An Introduction to Faith and Culture*, London: Darton, Longman, Todd, 1997.

Gallagher, M.P. and Whelan, C.T., 'Religious and Moral Values' in C.T. Whelan (ed.) *Values and Social Change in Ireland*, Dublin: Gill & Macmillan, 1994.

Lynch, K., *The Hidden Curriculum Reproduction in Education: An Appraisal*, London: Falmer, 1989.

Sarason, S., *Revisiting 'The Culture of the School and the Problem of Change'*, New York: Columbia Teachers' College Press, 1996.

Tuohy, D. *Leading Life to the Full*, Dublin: Veritas, 2005.

Tuohy, D. and Cairns, P., *Youth 2K: Threat or Promise to a Religious Culture?*, Dublin: Marino, 2000.

Tuohy, D. and Coghlan, D., 'Challenges of Educational Leadership: Meaning, Community and Excellence' in M. Fehenny (ed.) *From Ideal to Action: The Inner Nature of a Catholic School Today*, Dublin: Veritas, 1998.

Vatican, *The Religious Dimension of Education in a Catholic School*, 1988.

Vatican, *The Catholic School on the Threshold of the Third Millennium*, 1998.

Trusteeship of Schools: Some Perspectives

Mary Reynolds

INTRODUCTION

In this paper, I intend to present 'some perspectives on trusteeship'. Any consideration of educational trusteeship presupposes a number of premises:

- Education in a democracy is a shared/contested space;
- 'The child's name is now'– educational outcomes must optimise pupils' possibilities;
- Schooling and education involve the partnership and involvement of differing stakeholders with varying roles and responsibilities, mandates and accountability;
- Schools are a locus for influence;
- Philosophies underpinning education are becoming more diversified and radical change is happening in both policies and practice within education;
- Church interests need to clarify its mission in this change context now and into the future.

For the purpose of this paper, I will address trusteeship in the context of the Catholic voluntary school in the Republic of Ireland, mainly as it relates to schools held by religious congregations, with a brief reference to primary school trusteeship. While my focus is primarily on the development of trusteeship within voluntary secondary schools, the development of trusteeship is not restricted to this sector of schools, though it is the principal school sector owned by and under the trusteeship of religious today. Rather, it is a model for trusteeship engagement in other sectors and areas of education. Thus, for example, grammar school trusteeship is not significantly different, nor indeed is the exercise of proactive trusteeship in Church primary and post-primary schools north and south. It is about enhancement and the structures supporting that enhancement.

To return to my focus on the future of trusteeship of schools under religious trusteeship, at present there are approximately 380 voluntary Catholic schools in the Republic of Ireland, 30 of which are diocesan colleges and 350 of which are in the Trusteeship of Religious Congregations.

In addition within diocesan networks, a small number of primary schools are run by Religious Congregations and are described as convent and monastery schools. All the primary schools in a diocese, including convent and monastery schools, are under the patronage of the bishop of the diocese. Thus, convent and monastery primary schools either in diocesan or congregational property are integral to the overall provision of Catholic primary schools within a diocese. Congregational primary schools are supported by the congregational trustees in respect of the philosophy of education, services from education offices, policy development, for example admissions, and formation of staff and parents.

TRUSTEESHIP

While Religious Congregations have always exercised trusteeship in relation to the schools with which they are associated, the term 'trustee' was rarely used in relation to schools before 1970, when it became central to the emergence of the community school model. In the early 1990s CORI set about agreeing a definition of trusteeship that would make it clear that:

- The trust relates to Catholic education to which 'each congregation brings the richness of its original charism'.[1]
- There is a firm legal basis for the trustee role;
- Decisions about the future of the school rest ultimately with the trustees, albeit after extensive consultation.

Up to the 1970s, the voluntary Catholic school was the main provider of second-level education in Ireland, but this changed with the establishment of a state-run second-level system around that time. Voluntary school providers had then to ask themselves what was their specific identity in the overall system. This led to the conviction of the value and indeed the necessity of securing the future of a dynamic, independent, voluntary Catholic system of education which would provide a quality service to the parents and young people of Ireland. It was also increasingly realised that in the context of the unprecedented societal, political, economic and educational change of the period, there was a need for a purposeful exercise of trusteeship within a faith context, and that failure in this regard could lead to the demise of the sector. This concern gave rise to the concept articulated by CORI of the 'proactive trusteeship' who would at the same time provide ongoing support to schools in managing change and challenge schools to constantly re-visit and re-interpret the mission of the school and its policies in an open, reflective and dynamic fashion. *A Handbook for Leaders of Religious Congregations*, referred to as the 'Trustee Handbook', was published in 1996. Not only did this contain a formal definition of 'trusteeship', incorporating the elements already referred to, but it also provided a framework for a strong, effective, focused operational relationship between trustees and the other educational partners.

At a series of assemblies and other meetings in the mid-1990s, the members of CORI took on board the new emerging understanding of trusteeship, but also recognised that the opportunities associated with trusteeship would only be realised in situations in which trustees can:

- Articulate clearly the distinctive values and principles of their religious and educational philosophy;
- Engage proactively with the school to promote the philosophy and monitor the extent to which it is being implemented;
- Intervene in situations in which there is a departure from that philosophy.[2]

(Proposition formally adopted by CORI Assembly, 1994)

The formal adoption of this proposition was important because:

- It signalled a commitment on the part of the congregations to the continued existence of a network of voluntary secondary schools;
- It made clear that only in the context of the three conditions outlined above being met was it worth trying to maintain the voluntary and Catholic status of the schools.

The importance that congregations began to attach to trusteeship in the mid-1990s has been re-enforced by developments in national policy in recent years. In particular there is now:

- A consensus that the most appropriate way of accommodating the growing pluralism in society is the provision of diversity of school type;
- A commitment to enable parents to choose schools that reflect their religious, ethical and cultural values;
- Recognition in legislation that trustees are crucial in ensuring that there is clarity about the values that underpin the philosophy and ethos that each school is trying to promote and between which parents can exercise choice.

THE NEED FOR NEW FORMS OF TRUSTEESHIP

An awareness of the importance of trusteeship continues to grow, as does the realisation that existing arrangements for trusteeship need to change. Two of the main factors that gave rise to the need for change can be identified:

1 First is the idea that Catholic education is the responsibility of the whole Catholic community. It became increasingly clear that a situation in which parents and lay teachers were excluded from key positions in schools was not consistent with the thinking that emerged from the Second Vatican Council. Thus, having appointed a growing number of principals and established representative Boards of Management in most of their schools, congregations recognised that the involvement of lay people in trusteeship was the next logical step.

2 Second, there has been a sharp decline in the number of clerics and religious directly engaged in education and in the number of clerical and religious vocations. Simultaneously, religious in Ireland, many of whom are in the process of re-organisation at national and international level, are seeking new ways of exercising the trusteeship of schools. Congregations are exploring new ways forward; to build on the best of what has been, while seeking to create contemporary models of patronage, trusteeship, management and delivery of quality Catholic education, in fidelity to their founding charism.

PRESENT SITUATION

Many congregations are now engaged, in some instances collaboratively, in a process of exploration and planning for new forms of trusteeship. It is envisaged that such new structures will be based on Boards of Trustees, established as Charitable Trusts or Trust Companies, comprised in whole or in part of lay people, to which Religious Congregations could transfer some or all of their responsibilities. Much work is in process as to how such bodies might be legally constituted and how their composition would reflect the interests of all including:

- Safeguarding the religious tradition on which the school was founded – this is to recognise the gift of the spirit that was the founding intention within a particular context of faith and culture, a gift that is ever renewable, finding new expression for the enhancement of the school community;
- The ecclesial interest of safeguarding the Catholic nature of the school.

CORI is also exploring the idea of a Trust Representative Body. This would act as an umbrella group to all such trusts and would carry several responsibilities, including that of stewardship in regard to fidelity of the member trusts to the expressed values and Catholic character of the school. The vision informing this umbrella body, which would desirably be an influential, values-driven leadership body, is to assure quality Catholic education by the empowerment of Catholic school trusts.

NEW CHALLENGES

For the remainder of this paper, I wish to highlight some challenges that this time of transition to new trusteeship structures presents, particularly in the context of the Catholic school being part of the evangelising mission of the Church. Because of it being part of that mission, its operation entails an appropriate ecclesiology, including canonical considerations, a proper theology of mission and an understanding of community.

The People of God: The Church

Later in this paper, I will refer to some of the challenges which the juridical (canonical) approach to defining Catholic schooling raises. I would like first to acknowledge that the vision of Catholic school has been greatly enriched in a variety of official Church documents issued during and since the Second Vatican Council. Among those are:

- *Second Vatican Council: Declaration on Christian Education*;
- The Catholic School, *Gravissium educationis*, 1965;
- *The Religious Dimension of Education in a Catholic School*, 1988;
- Pope John Paul II, *Cathechesi tradedae*;
- *The Catholic School on the Threshold of the Third Millennium: Vatican Congregation for Catholic Education*, 2002.

These documents present a vision of Catholic education that promotes the idea of the Catholic school in dialogue with the modern world, claiming the right in that dialogue to speak 'meaningfully and imaginatively about the mystery of God – in the face of modernity and … of post modernity'.[3]

They highlight the distinguishing characteristics of the Catholic school that include:

- The specifically Christian view of the human person and society – an anthropology;
- An invitation to Christian faith and commitment in a life centred on Jesus and his values. The school is potentially a significant locus for pre-evangelisation, evangelisation/ catechesis for all members of the school community, for example pupils, families, staff and local community;
- The dialogue between faith and culture, promoting the critical assimilation of culture;
- The development of critical thinking, discernment and moral judgement;
- The community dimension of the school itself and its relationship with the wider community;
- The special concern for those who are weakest – socially, economically and spiritually;
- The school at the service of society and the common good.

The passing on of trusteeship to new Boards of Trusteeships will involve considerably more than handing on rights and powers, or providing legal frameworks and financial support. The challenge in calling lay people into the role of trusteeship involves the training and formation of those trustees in a vision of Catholic education. Opportunity for some formation in theology and spirituality in dialogue with education will be needed not just for trustees, but for those at the 'pit face', so to speak. The partners in educational provision at all levels – governance, management, teaching, pastoral care, outreach, quality delivery, support services – need formation and the capacity for faith-informed discernment if the exercise of trusteeship of Catholic education is to be promoted in fidelity and integrity within the Church and its faith community.

THEOLOGY OF MISSION

With the proposed change in trustee structures, there is an opportunity to formulate a theological formation of trusteeship that will come from a Theology of Baptism rather than the Theology of Religious Life. For many congregations, the educational ministry was an expression of their charism, a gift to the Church for the building of the Kingdom, which while situated in a particular context also evolved in its mode of expression. Hence a congregation whose charism emphasised a care for poor people might establish schools for the education of children of poor families. The congregational leadership, serving as trustees of those schools, were the guardians of the charism, tradition and heritage. After the Second Vatican Council and stemming from an emphasis on the universal call to holiness, there was an impetus to invite and engage laity in increasingly significant roles in some Church ministries. On the premise that Catholic education is a responsibility of the whole Catholic community, perhaps now is the time to articulate trusteeship of Catholic voluntary schools as a form of ministry in the Church. This would situate the responsibility of trusteeship within the evangelising mission of the Church itself and the ministry of trusteeship now under the aegis of a particular congregation would become one of the defined ministries with the Church. The reframing of the trusteeship role as a unique call in the Church would open the door to the thinking of trusteeship in a new way. It would also raise questions about, for example, how individuals might respond to this call, how they should prepare to minister in this role and how the wider community might create a community of people supporting those in the role of trustee for the mission of education.

COMMUNITY

Reframing the trusteeship concept as a specific ministry would require the identification of a supportive community for those who take on a trustee role. As lay persons begin to assume responsibility for the Catholic education ministry, they will not have available to them the supportive communities enjoyed by yesterday's/today's trustees. Something will need to fill the void. The Trustee Representative Body, envisioned by CORI, would provide part of this support, but the development of a sense of responsibility in the wider Catholic community for the ministry of Catholic education will be necessary. The document *The Catholic School on the Threshold of the Third Millennium* points out that it is 'urgent to sensitise Parochial and Diocesan communities to the necessity of their developing special care for education and schools'.

Another opportunity provided by this transition time is facilitating school communities – parents, staff, management and pupils – in knowing and owning their identity as Catholic schools and engaging in discussions around some fundamental questions. Among those questions might be:

1   In the pluralist context of Irish society today, what provision is necessary to ensure choice and availability for those who want Catholic schooling?

2   What commitment and support is there in the school community to give expression to the Catholic identity of the schools in its management, development, policies, curriculum and service?

3   What commitment and support is there in the wider community for the running of the Catholic voluntary school?

4   What distinctive contribution does the Catholic voluntary school offer to the education system as a whole?

The opportunity to refocus the identity of the Catholic voluntary school and to commit to ownership of it by the wider Catholic community and by the school community may indeed prove to be a movement of renewal and rebirth.

ISSUES OF CANON LAW

Part of the preparation for the new structures of trusteeship has been the exploration of canonical considerations and Civil Law Trust Models such as Charitable Trusts and Trust Companies. One of the guiding principles in law is its capacity to protect core values; this is central to all our explorations. Law cannot be separated from a value base, and I suggest there is a hierarchy of values to be considered. The question 'Why?' must inform all explorations.

A Catholic school is understood to be one which is under the control of the competent ecclesiastical authority of a public ecclesiastical juridical person or one which in a written document is acknowledged as Catholic by the ecclesiastical authority (C. 803 §1).

Religious Congregations are recognised as public juridic persons. Therefore, as trustees they fulfil the canonical requirement that a Catholic school be under the control of a public ecclesiastical juridic person. (This is not to overlook the role of local ordinaries and the responsibility for Catholic education within the diocesan jurisdiction.) The proposal to establish lay trustee bodies has raised the question of the juridic person in the future.

CORI has been exploring this and at this point is considering a number of possible scenarios:

- The concept of Trusteeship of Property for Mission;
- The idea of Associations of the Christian Faithful (ACFs);
- The creation of a Prelature for the Mission of Education within the island of Ireland.

Association of the Christian Faithful

1 The concept of Trusteeship of Property for Mission is based on Canon 115, which refers to an aggregate of goods being constituted as a juridic person (JP). This could provide the possibility of creating a juridic person based on the property of the schools to be used for the furtherance of mission of Catholic education. CORI have begun to explore this possibility;

2 The concept of Association of the Christian Faithful is explained in Canon 290 §1 as follows:

In the Church there are associations in which the Christian faithful strive by common effort:

- To promote a more perfect life;
- To foster public worship or Christian doctrine;
- To exercise other apostolic works, namely:
- To engage in evangelisation;
- To exercise works of piety or charity;
- To animate the temporal order with the Christian spirit.

It would seem that trusteeship of Catholic Schools would fit under this definition.

However, the question of Canonical Juridical Personality of ACFs is relevant to the exploration.

- A public association of the Christian faithful is established by the bishop (for his own territory), Episcopal Conference (in its territory for national associations) or Holy See (for universal and international associations). The decree which establishes it makes it *a public juridical person* and gives it its mission in the Church;
- A private association of the Christian faithful can be established by agreement among themselves. Canon 299 §1 says that Christ's faithful have the right to constitute associations for the purpose mentioned in Canon 290 (above). Such associations, once endorsed by the competent ecclesiastical authority, are recognised as private ACFs. A private ACF could become *a public juridical person* by decree of the appropriate ecclesial authority. This acquisition of juridical personality does not alter the private status of the association (C. 322 §1).

THE PROPERTY OF JURIDIC PERSON

- The temporal goods of a private JP are not considered to be 'ecclesiastical goods' (C. 1257 §2). Therefore, outright transfer of the property (buildings and lands) of a religious congregation to a private JP would be deemed to be alienation of Church property;
- The temporal goods of a public JP are 'ecclesiastical goods' (C. 1257 §1). Outright transfer of the property (buildings and lands) of a religious congregation to a public JP would not be alienation of Church property.

Possible Scenarios

A religious congregation might decide:
- To seek to have a Charitable Trust or Trust Company established by the competent authority as a public ACF (as a

public ACF it will have public juridic personality and a Religious Congregation, with canonical approval, would be able to make an outright transfer of property to it);

- To establish a Charitable Trust or Trust Company as a private ACF which may have either public or private juridic personality and the Religious Congregation, with canonical approval, will have the option to either licence their property to it (if it has private juridical personality) or lease or make an outright transfer of property to it (if it has public juridical personality).

But public and private ACFs require vigilance of competent ecclesiastical authority. The ecclesiastical supervision of public and private ACFs canonically required (C. 305) has a twofold purpose:

1 Preservation of integrity of faith;
2 Verification by the authority that there is no abuse of ecclesiastical discipline.

However, the implications of setting up a considerable number of Catholic schools trusts, each holding a large number of schools, would be enormous for the Conference of Bishops (CoB). Moreover, the CoB does not have the structures to deal with the canonical requirements relative to vigilance over public and private ACFs and relative to accountability. The CoB could be served in this by a National Education Service for Catholic Schools such as exists in other jurisdictions. The Trust Representative Body as proposed by CORI could be structured in a way that might answer this need.

I have referred already to the Trust Representative Body as a possible umbrella trust with a stewardship role towards participating Trusts. It may be possible to establish the TRB also as a Public Juridic Person. Canon 313 states:

A public association as well as a confederation of public associations is constituted a juridic person by the decree by what it is erected by a competent ecclesiastic authority in accord with the norm of C. 312.

There is also a facility within Canon Law for establishing as part of the National Episcopal Conference, a prelature for a particular mission, which is not a personal prelature. Perhaps such a prelature for the mission of education in Ireland might be worth exploring.

CONCLUSION

Religious Congregations do not envisage the handing over of trusteeship of schools as a 'closing down', but rather the passing on of something that they have pioneered and developed. The handing over, which is likely to be a gradual process rather than a once-off event, is full of opportunity for empowerment and partnership. To engage with future lay trustees in developing a theological foundation for trusteeship, to co-devise with them the formational, educational and training opportunities to meet their needs as they take up their role, to explore the canonical and legal structures that allow them to assume public trust of the education ministry and to raise the awareness of the Catholic community to their responsibility for Catholic education is an exciting and enriching project. This is a time when congregations can be heroically generative as they transition their legacy to new forms and empower and trust others to bring it forward.

It is a time too for congregations to be collaborative in their approach to the provision of Catholic education. All the education traditions of the Religious Congregations, while uniquely important in a local context of ministry, collectively continue the teaching ministry of Jesus. What matters to those who will be trustees of the Catholic education ministry in the future is that Gospel values will underpin their educational enterprise. Hopefully the tradition of the congregations who initiated and shaped the development of the enterprise will continue to influence, but that is secondary to the continuation of a Catholic sector of education, based on a Gospel-inspired philosophy. In her book *Wrestling with God,* Barbara Fiand passionately asserts that congregational protectionism cannot have a place in a world called to radical transformation. The following quotation captures the challenge facing us in our collaborative efforts:

> The same spirit that led women and men religious to begin new works, to establish new facilities and to launch new ministries, flourishes in the Church today. The charism of each Religious Congregation is from one Spirit, a gift to be given, to be used, to be spent. It is an evolving gifting to and from the Church. Ultimately, this post conciliar age is witnessing the emergence of new spiritual endowments, of new corporate forms with potentially stronger, more vital and viable ministries. In this time Congregations must re-vision, reassert and celebrate that which unites them rather than that which sets them apart.[4]

I once heard the poet Máirtin O'Direáin say that a poem was like standing on the middle of a bridge. It connects the creativity of the author and the creativity of the reader and out of that is born something greater than the writer ever imagined. In a sense we stand on the middle of a bridge, preparing to offer 'our poem' to those who will re-imagine it. The structure and the process for doing that will be all important.

Notes

1 Vatican Congregation on Education, *The Religious Dimension of Education in a Catholic School*, 1988.

2 CORI, *Handbook for Leaders of Religious Congregations*, 1977, Chapter 1, p. 12.

3 Dermot A. Lane, 'Afterword: The Expanding Horizons of Catholic Education' in P. Hogan and K. Williams (eds) *The Future of Religion in Irish Education*, Dublin: Veritas, 1977.

4 Barbara Fiand SND deN, *Wrestling with God*, New York: Crossroad Publishing, 1996.

The Ecclesial Dimension of Catholic Education

Archbishop J. Michael Miller

The subject of the future of Catholic schools in contemporary Ireland is of vital importance not only to those in the Emerald Isle but also to the universal Church, which looks to them for inspiration as a society enlightened by more than fifteen hundred years of living the Catholic faith, often amidst the most trying of circumstances.

For twenty years, I was engaged in this apostolate, primarily at the tertiary but also at the secondary level. I have a passion for Catholic education and all that it can offer to the new evangelisation, which is the way of the Church in this first century of the third Christian millennium. Without making light of the challenges, even the downright difficulties, that characterise the present situation of possessive individualism, privatisation of faith, clerical scandals and decline in sacramental practice, you have in your hands – to shape with a potter's dexterity – an irreplaceable instrument for keeping the Gospel alive in the heart of Ireland: your Catholic school system.

I hope that this paper will encourage you in your common endeavour and, perhaps, even provide some considerations that will help you to move forward with courage to take the next steps in the unity of the Spirit.

THE CHURCH'S ENGAGEMENT IN EDUCATION

By her nature, the Church has the right and the duty to proclaim the Gospel to all nations.[1] Education belongs to the Church's prophetic vocation. It is an integral dimension of her mission of evangelisation, of inviting people to Christ and the fullness of an ecclesial, sacramental life. In the history of the Church, different cultures and political systems have given rise to a wide variety of educational institutions to meet this responsibility. Bishops, religious communities and parents have courageously explored creative ways of educating children and young people in various local churches.

Fundamental to all Catholic education is the task of forming the faithful in their knowledge and practice of the faith. This has been, and undoubtedly remains, the case in Ireland. Only recently have schools begun to serve other members of an increasingly multi-cultural and pluralistic society. In many countries of Asia and Africa, and to a lesser degree certain regions of the United States and Canada, service to non-Catholics and non-Christians has long been known in many Catholic schools. How this particular service can best be carried out in the 'new Ireland' has not yet been fully worked out, especially at the primary level.

Among the many means of educating the faithful, one that has been particularly fruitful in the last few centuries is the Catholic school. In numerous nations, including Ireland, 'Catholic elementary schools ... have been instrumental in educating successive generations of Catholics, and in teaching the truths of the faith, promoting respect for the human person, and developing the moral character of their students'.[2] Complementing the home and parish, they have been the backbone of handing on the faith to Catholic children, preparing them for the sacraments and providing a healthy Christian atmosphere for their human and spiritual development. The rapidity with which the religious practice in Ireland has declined is a great challenge to Catholic schools today, adding a new evangelisation to their mission, which reaches out to Catholic children whose contact with the Church is tenuous or even non-existent.

Irish Catholic schools have an illustrious history. Founded for the most part by consecrated women and men who dedicated their lives to the education of young people, they arose as an ecclesial response to foster the life of faith and the progress of society. One needs only mention the names of Catherine McAuley, Edmund Rice or Nano Nagle to bring to mind the extraordinary influence that religious women and men have had on Irish culture and Church life through their network of primary and secondary schools. Your purpose in sponsoring this historical meeting at this time of *kairos*, this moment of decision and grace, is to plan intentionally how to continue that great tradition. It must be faithfully and creatively adapted to contemporary circumstances, in light of the changes that have occurred in recent decades, especially the secularisation of the culture, the precipitous decline in the number of religious in the schools and the blessing of the laity's increasing role in Catholic education.

FIVE ESSENTIAL 'MARKS' OF CATHOLIC SCHOOLS

While taking into account the particular nature of Ireland's confrontation with postmodernity, the Church proposes certain constant elements in her teaching about the specific ethos of Catholic schools. Like the 'marks' of the Church proclaimed in the Creed, so, too, can we identify the principal 'ideal' characteristics of a school *qua Catholic*. I will expand the four ecclesial marks to five scholastic ones! Catholic schools proceed *ex corde Ecclesiae*, from the very heart of the Church – both universal and local.

As the Holy Father recently reminded a group of bishops on their *ad limina* visit: 'It is of utmost importance, therefore, that the Church's institutions be genuinely Catholic: Catholic in their self-understanding and Catholic in their identity. All those who share in the apostolates of such institutions, including those who are not of the faith, should show a sincere and respectful appreciation of that mission which is their inspiration and ultimate *raison d'être*.[3] It is precisely because of its Catholic ethos, which is anything but narrowly sectarian, that a school derives the originality enabling it to be a genuine instrument of the Church's apostolic mission.[4] Let's, then, look at these five non-negotiables of Catholic identity, the lofty ideals that inspire the Church's enormous investment in schooling.

Inspired by a Supernatural Vision

The enduring foundation on which the Church builds her educational philosophy is her conviction that it is a process which forms the integral human person, especially in their transcendence, with eyes fixed on the vision of God.[5] The specific purpose of a Catholic education is the formation of students who will be good citizens of this world, enriching society with the leaven of the Gospel, but who are also being prepared to become citizens of the world to come. As Vatican II's *Declaration on Catholic Education*, whose fortieth anniversary we are celebrating this year, states so clearly:

> The Catholic school, while it is open, as it must be, to the situation of the contemporary world, leads its students to promote efficaciously the good of the earthly city and also prepares them for service in the spread of the Kingdom of God, so that by leading an exemplary apostolic life they become, as it were, a saving leaven in the human community.[6]

An emphasis on the inalienable dignity of the human person, above all on their spiritual dimension, is especially necessary today when so many in government, business, the media and even the educational establishment itself perceive education to be merely an instrument for the acquisition of information which will improve the chances of worldly success and a more comfortable standard of living.

In a speech addressed to Catholic educators, Pope John Paul II presents all of us, including Irish educators, with

> the pressing challenge of clearly identifying the aims of Catholic education, and applying proper methods in Catholic elementary and secondary education ... It is the challenge of fully understanding the educational enterprise, of properly evaluating its content, and of transmitting the full truth concerning the human person, created in God's image and called to life in Christ through the Holy Spirit.[7] If we fail to keep in mind this high supernatural vision, all our talk about Catholic schools will be no more than 'a gong booming or a cymbal clashing' (I Cor 13:1). *(Address to Catholic Educators, New Orleans, 12 September, 1987, 7)*

Focused on Christ

Inspired by this transcendent goal, a second mark of Catholic education is its radically Christological focus. In 1977 the Holy See published its first document on Catholic schools, appropriately titled *The Catholic School*, a document which still retains all its vitality and freshness – required reading for all of us. It insists that, to be worthy of its name, a Catholic school must be founded on 'a Christian concept of life centred on Jesus Christ'[8] the Redeemer who, through his Incarnation, is united with each student. Christ is not an after-thought or an add-on to Catholic educational philosophy but the centre and fulcrum of the entire enterprise, the light enlightening every pupil who comes into our schools (cf. Jn 1:9). In this document the congregation stated:

> The Catholic school is committed thus to the development of the whole man, since in Christ, the

perfect man, all human values find their fulfilment and unity. Herein lies the specifically Catholic character of the school. Its duty to cultivate human values in their own legitimate right in accordance with its particular mission to serve all men has its origin in the figure of Christ. He is the one who ennobles man, gives meaning to human life, and is the model which the Catholic school offers to its pupils.[9]

Students, therefore, should be helped to find the inspiration for their daily lives in the words and the example of Jesus, conversing with him in prayer and receiving him in the Eucharist.

That Christ is the 'one foundation' of Catholic schools is surely not news to anyone here. But this conviction, in its very simplicity, can sometimes be overlooked. Indeed, unfortunately, we can no longer automatically assume, without further examination, that all those associated with Catholic schools – administrators, teachers, trustees and parents – recognise this fundamental Christological principle.

Permeated by a Catholic Worldview
A third characteristic of Catholic schools might sound like a truism: the 'spirit of Catholicism' should permeate the entire curriculum, not just the class period of religious education or the school's pastoral activities. Instruction should be authentically Catholic in content and methodology across the curriculum. Even sound religious education can be undermined by what is taught in biology, history or literature courses.

I am convinced that Catholicism has a particular 'take' on reality that should animate its schools. Scott Appleby has written:

The challenge of Catholic education and formation in our media-driven, cyberspace age is no less than this: Older Catholics must be restored to and younger

68

Catholics introduced to a sense of Catholicism as a comprehensive way of life – as a comprehending wisdom and set of practices that bring integrity and holiness to individuals and to the families and extended communities to which they belong and which they serve.[10]

This 'comprehensive way of life' has both an intellectual and a devotional component. The first entails the Catholic emphasis on synthesising faith and culture; the second touches on the incarnational–sacramental understanding of reality, which is the basis of what Rosemary Haughton once called 'the Catholic thing'.

If Catholic education is to respond to the challenges of the twenty-first century, it must ensure that its ethos fosters these profound convictions about how we grasp and treat reality. Catholic schools are responsible for putting flesh on these attitudinal bones.

Learning, Faith and Truth
An insight governing all Catholic education from the apostolic age down to the present is the notion that faith requires learning for it to be lively, engaging and ultimately transformative of the whole person and of society. Catholics trace their intellectual lineage to those thinkers who teach that reason is compatible with faith, and they have embraced the school apostolate to teach truths about nature, human existence, society, the universe and God.

This distinctive feature of our Catholic intellectual tradition is the conviction – and in this it departs from some forms of Protestantism which has exalted faith at the expense of reason – that acquiring knowledge through reason and knowledge through faith are both valid and ultimately compatible, even if not identical. Faith presupposes and completes reason. Even today this belief in the unity of truth continues to undergird Catholic thinking at every level.

In a 1997 document calling for the courageous renewal of Catholic schools, the Congregation for Catholic Education commented:

> The endeavour to interweave reason and faith, which has become the heart of individual subjects, makes for unity, articulation and coordination, bringing forth within what is learnt in a school a Christian vision of the world, of life, of culture and of history ... All of this demands an atmosphere characterized by the search for truth, in which competent, convinced and coherent educators, teachers of learning and life, may be a reflection, albeit imperfect but still vivid, of the one Teacher.[11]

Intrinsically related to this notion of the compatibility of faith and reason is another principle of our tradition – that of truth. Unlike sceptics and relativists, Catholic teachers share a specific conviction about truth: that it can be pursued and, to a limited but real extent, attained by the human mind.

Truth matters. Catholic educators have 'a passion for truth'. Even if some might argue that such a position smacks of arrogance, education 'in the truth' is proper to our apostolate, for it is only when freedom is linked to truth that a society has the solid foundation necessary for a strong democracy.

Incarnational–Sacramental Vision

As well as sharing these strong beliefs about truth and the harmony of faith and reason, Ireland's Catholic schools of the twenty-first century must also keep paying attention to another aspect of a specifically Catholic view of reality: that which stresses the world's incarnational and sacramental dimension.

As a historical religion, Catholicism is rooted in the foundational events of Jesus' birth, ministry, death and resurrection. We accept the testimony of those who heard, looked upon and even touched the Word of life (cf. I Jn 1:1). Catholic schools must take seriously this mystery of the Incarnation, the Son's living the adventure of human life among us.

It is crucial, then, that administrators, pastors, parents, trustees and teachers 'get it right' on this essential point. The entire pontificate of Pope John Paul II – from his first encyclical *Redemptor hominis* to his proclamation of this Year of the Eucharist – has been, and is, a sustained catechesis on the mystery of Christ: on who he is, on what he has done, and on the implications for his followers of what it means to believe in him. The flourishing of third millennial Irish Catholicism depends in large measure on the extent to which Catholic schools embrace the Incarnation as the truth that grounds their ecclesial and social service.

The Incarnation, which emphasises the *bodily* coming of God's Son into the world, leaves its seal on every aspect of Christian life. In a Catholic worldview, which the school curriculum is to foster in all its parts, the created cosmos bridges the gap between God and humanity. The very fact of the Incarnation tells us that the created world is the means chosen by God through which he communicates his life to us. What is human and visible is capable of bearing the divine.

If Catholic schools are to be authentic, they should make every effort to suffuse their environment with this delight in the sacramental. Therefore, they should express physically and visibly the external signs of Catholic culture through images, signs, symbols, icons and other objects of traditional devotion. There should be space for at least a small chapel – the heart of the Catholic school – where students and teachers can go to pray and where they can find copies of sacred scripture, rosaries and reading materials, which will lead to reflection and foster genuine friendship with God.

Sustained by the Martyrology of Teaching

Catholic education is strengthened by its 'martyrs'. Like the early Church, it is built up through the shedding of their blood. Those of us who are, or have been, teachers know all about that. But I am speaking here about 'martyrs' in the original sense of 'witnesses'.

As well as fostering a Catholic view throughout the curriculum, even in so-called secular subjects, 'if students in Catholic schools are to gain a genuine experience of the Church, the example of teachers and others responsible for their formation is crucial: the witness of adults in the school community is a vital part of the school's identity'.[12] Children will pick up far more by example than by masterful pedagogical techniques, especially in the practice of Christian virtues. A school's ethos is the child's primary teacher.

Educators at every level in the Church are expected to be models for their students by bearing transparent witness to the Gospel. This is the fourth mark of our schools' ethos. Transmitting the rich fullness of Christian doctrine, though essential, is an insufficient measure of catholicity. If pupils are to experience the splendour of the Church, the Christian example of teachers and others responsible for their formation is crucial. This witness of adults in the school community is an integral component of a school's Catholic identity.

The prophetic words of Pope Paul VI ring as true today as they did thirty years ago: 'Modern man listens more willingly to witnesses than to teachers, and if he does listen to teachers, it is because they are witnesses.'[13] What teachers do and how they act are more significant than what they say – inside and outside the classroom. That is how the Church evangelises. 'The more completely an educator can give concrete witness to the model of the ideal person [Christ] that is being presented to the students, the more this ideal will be believed and imitated.'[14] Today's students are particularly turned off by hypocrisy. While their demands are high, perhaps sometimes even unreasonably so, there is no getting away from the fact that if teachers fail to model fidelity to the truth and virtuous behaviour, then even the best of curricula cannot successfully propose Christian values and promote a Catholic ethos.

Imbued by a Spirit of Prayer

The fifth and last mark of a school's Catholic identity is the extent to which it promotes holiness through the strong liturgical and prayer life of its teachers and pupils. Central to the Catholic school is its mission of holiness. In a discourse to the Irish Christian Brothers, Pope John Paul II recalled that 'Edmund [Rice] showed himself faithful to the ancient tradition of the great monastic schools of Ireland which had forged a profound link between sanctity and learning, humanity and education, to the glory of Europe and the entire Christian world'.[15] Mindful of our redemption in Christ, the Catholic school aims at forming in its pupils those particular virtues that will enable them to live a new life in Christ and help them to play faithfully their part in building up the Kingdom of God.[16]

Prayer should be a normal part of the day, not just a rote recitation, so that students learn to pray in times of sorrow and joy, of disappointment and celebration, of difficulty and success. Especially the sacraments of the Eucharist and Reconciliation should mark the rhythm of a Catholic school's life. Mass ought to be celebrated regularly, with the students and teachers participating appropriately. Traditional Catholic devotions should also have their place, such as praying the rosary, decorating May altars, singing hymns, reading from the Bible and lives of the saints, and celebrating the rhythm of the Church's liturgical year. Days of retreat and reflection both for students and teachers also contribute greatly to deepening their life of prayer and their personal relationship with the Lord. The vitality of the Catholic faith is expressed in these and similar acts of religion which belong to everyday ecclesial life.

While the Religious Education Department has a very significant influence on a school's overall Catholic ethos, this is not its responsibility alone.[17] Even so, its staff members do have a special role to play. They can assist teachers in other departments by suggesting ways to incorporate the Catholic ethos into classroom activities, and they can help their colleagues look for opportunities to integrate 'the Catholic thing' into the material content of their lessons.

WHO IS RESPONSIBLE FOR CATHOLIC EDUCATION?

Having considered the essential dimensions of what makes a school Catholic, I would now like to turn to a more difficult and practical consideration. At this point it might be helpful to ask the question: Who is responsible for Catholic education in Ireland? Before answering this, however, I would like to sketch the ecclesial context that is the basis of an adequate response: the ecclesiology of communion proposed by the Second Vatican Council.

Catholic Schools and the Mystery of 'Koinonia'

The Triune God reveals himself as a mystery of communion of persons and calls us to enter into communion with him and with one another so that we may have 'life to the full' (cf. Jn 10:10; I Jn 1:3). 'To make the Church the home and the school of communion: that is the great challenge facing us in the millennium which is now beginning', the Holy Father has affirmed. But what does this mean, in practice, for a school system? The Pope replied:

> Let us have no illusions: unless we follow external structures of communion will serve very little purpose. They would become mechanisms without a soul, 'masks' of communion rather than its means of expression and growth.[18]

All those involved in Catholic educational endeavours – from bishops to religious, from administrators to teachers, from public officials to trustees, from parents to pupils – are invited to carry out their mission in this spirit of communion. Indeed, all efforts to revitalise and hand on genuinely Catholic schools will come to naught unless they are carried out with this profound sense of ecclesial communion, which presupposes collaboration but rises far above it. Sustaining and promoting the lively network of Ireland's Catholic schools depends on selfless and engaged cooperation, without which 'we can do nothing' (cf. Jn 15:5).

Parents

Who, then, bears the awesome, if sometimes burdensome, task of being responsible for educating our children and young people? Church teaching is clear. The Second Vatican Council declared that, 'since parents have conferred life on their children, they have a most solemn obligation to educate their offspring. Hence, parents must be acknowledged as the first and foremost educators of their children'.[19] Their responsibility is 'irreplaceable and inalienable, and therefore incapable of being entirely delegated to others or usurped by others'.[20] Indeed, this obligation is rooted in the sacrament of marriage, which bestows on parents the grace necessary to accomplish this awesome task. Catholic schools are, therefore, trustees of other people's children.

Parents delegate to the school, whether State or Church controlled, a share in their responsibility. Catholic schools are only helpmates in this undertaking. No school system can ever override the firm Catholic conviction that 'parents have been appointed by God himself as the first and principal educators of their children and that their right is completely inalienable'.[21]

In helping the family fulfil its obligation, civil society also has certain rights and duties. Its role is to promote the common good, especially through the support of educational institutions according to the wishes of the families. In a special way, however, the duty of educating is an ecclesial responsibility: 'The Church is bound as a mother to give to these children of hers an education by which their whole life can be imbued with the spirit of Christ.'[22]

It is this last responsibility, that belonging to the Church, that is our particular interest: *Who* in the Church is responsible and in what way?

Bishops

The Catholic school should play a vital role in the pastoral activity of the diocese.[23] It is a pastoral instrument of the Church for her mission of evangelisation. The bishop's pastoral leadership is pivotal in lending support and guidance to Catholic schools. Indeed, 'only the bishop can set the tone, ensure the priority and effectively present the importance of the cause to the Catholic people'.[24]

The bishop's responsibility for Catholic education, and for Catholic schools in particular, is derived from the *munus docendi* received at ordination.[25] As the Code of Canon Law states: 'Pastors of souls have the duty of making all possible arrangements so that all the faithful may avail themselves of a Catholic education.'[26] With regard to Catholic schools, episcopal responsibility is twofold: first, integrating schools into the diocese's pastoral programme and, second, overseeing the teaching within them.

More than ever, Catholic life in Ireland needs what episcopal leadership alone can provide. A clear vision of the Church's educational mission is an irreplaceable aspect of being a pastor of the flock. Eschewing any indirection, the Pope affirms that 'bishops need to support and enhance the work of Catholic schools'.[27]

Establishing Schools

In order to help parents meet their obligation of giving their children a Catholic education, the Church's pastors have the responsibility of providing the instruments to accomplish this. While Catholic schools are the most effective way to educate large numbers of children, other methods also deserve episcopal support, such as seeing to religious instruction in State schools or encouraging home schooling, a movement just taking root in Ireland.

Canon Law specifically encourages bishops to ensure that schools with a Christian spirit are established in their dioceses.[28] Often this means being attentive to where new schools are needed due to demographic shifts. Because of his responsibility for the spiritual life of the faithful, even – or especially – during the formative years of young people, it falls to the bishop to guarantee that schools with a Catholic ethos are made available for his flock, including those who are disabled, needy or require special attention.

According to Church law, for a school to be 'Catholic' it must be supervised by a public ecclesiastical juridic person, almost always, at least until now, a religious institute, or it must be overseen or recognised by ecclesiastical authority.[29] Furthermore, such a school is to provide a formation based on Catholic teaching, and its teachers are to be outstanding for their correct doctrine and integrity of life. This first point is relevant to our discussion. If a school is entrusted to an association whose board is composed primarily or totally of lay people, and if such an association lacks the status of a public ecclesiastical juridic person, it must receive the written approval of the bishop to operate a 'Catholic' school.

Munus Docendi: Transmitting Church Doctrine
Episcopal oversight also entails the bishop's overseeing that the education and formation in his schools are based on the principles of Catholic doctrine. This vigilance over Catholic schools includes even those established or directed by members of religious institutes.[30]

His particular responsibilities include ensuring that teachers are known to be sound in their doctrine and outstanding in their integrity of life.[31] Because of certain developments in the last thirty or forty years, this exercise of *episkope* must judge whether children are receiving the 'fullness' of the Church's faith.

In some local churches, though Ireland may well be an exception, a frequent challenge to sound doctrine in Catholic schools is not what is included, but what is left out. For example, textbooks or teachers that present Jesus as our brother, friend or model are not teaching anything against the faith. But if they do not in some appropriate way explain the fascination of his divine personhood, that is a serious crack in the foundation of Catholic doctrine. Or again, if baptism is presented only as the welcoming of a new Christian into the community of believers, the error is not in what is said but in what is omitted: the overwhelming mystery of the utter gratuity of divine mercy and the creedal confession of belief in 'one baptism for the forgiveness of sins'.

Equally important is the need for the bishop to supervise the religious and moral integrity of administrators and teachers. In short, those involved in Catholic schools, with very few exceptions, should be practising Catholics committed to the Church and living her sacramental life. I daresay that in Ireland the majority of teachers and other personnel in its Catholic schools are models of dedication grounded in the spiritual, intellectual and moral values of our tradition.

Despite the difficulties involved, it is, I believe, a serious mistake to be anything other than a 'rigorist' with regard to the personnel hired. The Catholic school system in Ontario, Canada, where I was raised, when pressured by public authorities for what they regarded as reasonable accommodations, relaxed this requirement for a time. The results were disastrous. With the influx of non-Catholic teachers into the schools, many of them ended up by seriously compromising their Catholic identity. Children 'picked up', even if they were not taught, a soft indifferentism which sustained neither their practice of the faith nor their ability to imbue society with authentically Christian values.[32]

Bishops, therefore, have a serious duty to see to the hiring of teachers who meet the standards of doctrine and integrity of life essential to maintaining and advancing a school's Catholic identity. The careful hiring of men and women who enthusiastically endorse a Catholic ethos is, I would say, the primary way in which their catholicity can be fostered. This care is particularly true for religious education teachers, where the right of the bishop to remove, or require to be removed, a teacher who fails to meet these standards is clearly stated in Church law.[33] But, I believe, this right also applies, by extension, to teachers of other subjects. Because of the legal situation in which we live today, bishops must make sure that the diocesan policy manual on employment, prudently and courageously making use of the relevant provisions of the 1998 Education Act, clearly states the requirement that all who work in Catholic schools must be living in accord with Church teaching and provides for the removal of the employee when the contrary has been proven.

It is important that the bishop be involved in Catholic schools not only by exercising veto power – whether over texts, curricula or teachers – but also that he be actively involved in the educational development of those entrusted to his pastoral care. Like good shepherds, bishops should above all encourage parents, teachers, students, priests and trustees to fulfil their obligations to Christ and the Church in the area of education. Some bishops, and some bishops' conferences, write pastoral letters about schools or sponsor Catholic Schools Week. Many bishops visit schools frequently for formal events or informal gatherings, or they invite students and teachers to the cathedral for special occasions. Short courses or retreats for teachers can be another point of contact between the school and the bishop.

Teachers and administrators always appreciate opportunities to speak personally to their bishop and express their hopes and concerns about pressing issues. The bishop can also foster a spirit of communion among families, parishes and schools through diocesan events, visits to parishes and schools, and the promotion of Catholic schools in organisations of parents, teachers, religious, clergy or other groups of the faithful.

In an *ad limina* address to a group of bishops in June 2004, the Holy Father summed up all that I have been trying to say. He told them that 'the Church's presence in elementary and secondary education must ... be the object of your special attention as shepherds of the People of God'.[34] In particular, pastors should set in place 'specific programmes of formation' which will enable the laity to take on responsibilities for teaching in Catholic schools.[35]

As your discussions continue on the establishment, composition and responsibilities of boards of trustees, I would suggest that the members be selected with utmost attention paid to their solid commitment to fostering the Catholic ethos of schools and to their genuine witness to the sacramental life. Moreover, the bishops ought always to be active partners in the conversation about the future of primary and secondary education in the Republic of Ireland and in Northern Ireland. The relationship between the bishop and the trustees should be a concrete expression of the school's ecclesial nature, where each individual fulfils his or her appropriate duties and is accorded his or her proper rights. Bishops are not 'external agents' to their Catholic schools, even those run by religious. Rather, they are active participants in their life, with specific responsibilities of oversight belonging to them as shepherds of their local Church.[36]

Religious
I would like to point out that the presence of religious 'continues to be indispensable in Catholic schools'.[37]

Consecrated women and men have a specific duty 'to bring to bear on the world of education their radical witness to the values of the Kingdom ... [They are] able to be especially effective in educational activities and to offer a specific contribution to the work of other educators'.[38]

Canon 801 calls on religious institutes with an apostolate in education to devote themselves to this mission through their schools established with the consent of the diocesan bishop. Catholic schools conducted by religious are, as Vatican II affirms, 'subject to the authority of the local Ordinaries for purposes of general policy-making and vigilance, but the right of religious to direct them remains intact'.[39]

In his post-synodal apostolic exhortation *Vita consecrata*, the Pope invited members of congregations devoted to education 'to be faithful to their founding charism and to their traditions, knowing that the preferential love for the poor finds a special application in the choice of means capable of freeing people from that grave form of poverty which is the lack of cultural and religious training'.[40]

Canon 678 §3 is particularly germane to this inter-conference meeting, charging bishops and religious superiors to work together in mutual consultation in directing apostolic works at the service of the Church. The Congregation for Bishops, in its recently updated *Directory for the Pastoral Ministry of Bishops* (2004), noted that:

> ... for the sake of improved co-ordination of different apostolic works and programmes within the diocesan pastoral context, and with a view to becoming better acquainted and fostering mutual esteem, it is good that the bishop should regularly meet the superiors of the institutes. This should provide an excellent opportunity for sharing experiences, identifying goals for evangelisation and finding suitable methods to meet the needs of the faithful.[41]

Meetings at the national level can provide information, contacts and inspiration for future gatherings at the local level which will be necessary to work out the details of the boards of trustees of individual schools. As the shepherd of his diocese, the bishop oversees Catholic schools so that they will contribute to building up his local Church.

The Lay Faithful

The future of Irish Catholic schools will be largely determined by lay women and men committed to the educational apostolate, which 'receives from the bishops in some manner the "mandate" of an apostolic undertaking'.[42]

More than a profession, teaching must be appreciated and lived as 'a supernatural Christian vocation'[43] if it is to take its place among properly ecclesial activities. Sometimes teachers undertake this apostolate consciously embracing, to the extent appropriate to their state of life, the charism of a particular religious institute, with all that involves by way of a specific spirituality and approach to pedagogy. It is certainly worthwhile for you to explore in greater depth the canonical forms, such as associations of the lay faithful, which could serve to guarantee the Catholic heritage of schools founded by religious congregations. While it is highly commendable that religious seek to hand on some elements of their particular charism to certain members of the laity, what is primary in all strategic planning for the future is safeguarding and promoting the Catholic ethos of Ireland's schools. After all, an institution is *first of all* Catholic, before it can be moulded according to a particular charism.

In light of Vatican II's teaching that 'lay people have their own proper competence in the building up of the Church'[44] I believe that lay men and women, precisely as members of the lay faithful, have their own 'charism of teaching', independent of the charism of a particular religious congregation. In the not too distant future, individual religious communities might die out, or they might flourish once again. What will definitely survive, we believe, is the Church herself – and her schools, which she can recognise as identifiably Catholic.

EDUCATIONAL STRUCTURES OF COMMUNION

As this inter-conference meeting testifies, the current situation in Ireland demands changes in the structures necessary to support and strengthen its Catholic schools, especially at the second level. Given the decreasing role of religious and the increasing involvement of bishops and laity in this endeavour, it seems likely that some existing organisations will need to be significantly enlarged and others created in order to guarantee their genuine catholicity, a catholicity marked by openness, conviction, creativity and a solid commitment to the high ideals of their specific ethos. I would like to emphasise that these are structures of communion inspired by principles enunciated at the Second Vatican Council. Bishops, religious, lay people, parents and trustees are co-responsible agents in fostering the school community. Together they plan and put into operation an educational project that is genuinely Catholic. The assigning of various responsibilities is governed by the principle of subsidiarity: the bishop recognises the competence of the professionals who, in turn, respect his pastoral authority.[45]

National Structures

It might prove useful to look at how some other episcopal conferences organise their educational apostolate. The websites of the Australian and American conferences offer a detailed look at their structures, their mission statements and the responsibilities of various commissions and committees. Catholic schools in both countries have a number of similarities to the situation in Ireland. I understand that, for more than a decade, CORI has dedicated a great deal of effort to studies of the structures in other countries. Such work can help enormously in guaranteeing the precious heritage of Irish Catholic schools. The experience of the Church in other countries can provide valuable insight into what structures work best and what pitfalls are to be avoided.

Almost every country has a national schools office, either within the structure of the episcopal conference or closely linked to it. The size and responsibilities range from the very extensive, in countries with a national educational system and numerous Catholic schools, to the very limited, where Catholic schools are few or dependent on widely divergent regional regulations.

In Ireland, the Department of Catholic Education and Formation already exists within the Irish Episcopal Conference. It might prove helpful in the future, though I instinctively react against burgeoning bureaucracies as a response to pastoral challenges, to enlarge the responsibilities of this commission. In any case, it could provide assistance to the dioceses in broader issues such as government policy, religious education, the permanent formation of teachers and trustees, and so on.

Regional Structures

Many countries also find regional offices to be helpful. This is the case where dioceses are small and cannot afford to have their own offices for certain responsibilities, or because they need to deal with regional legislation. For example, in the United States, although the national and diocesan offices are well developed, offices also exist at the state level to deal with legislation and government funding issues, which vary a great deal from one state to another. I do not know whether such regional structures would be a help or a hindrance in the Irish situation.

Diocesan Structures

Throughout the universal Church it is the common practice that any diocese with more than a few educational institutions has a diocesan office which oversees, on behalf of the Ordinary, that formation and education in his Catholic schools is, as the Code of Canon Law affirms, 'based on the principles of Catholic doctrine' and that the teachers are themselves 'outstanding in true doctrine and uprightness of life'.[46] Again, to take an example from Australia, such offices can be as large as the Catholic Education Office of the Archdiocese of Sydney, or as small as the one officer, one part-time secretary and four consultants of the Catholic Education Office in the diocese of Bunbury in remote Western Australia. Such offices can be a helpful expression of the episcopal oversight of Catholic education and, in a spirit of ecclesial communion, they can foster cooperation among religious, lay people and the bishop in their common endeavour at the local level.

CONCLUSION

The challenges facing Irish schools today require the serious discussion such as that we are having in these days. Inter-conference meetings are also an occasion to celebrate the great accomplishments of the past and to set a path of hope for the future. All of us – bishops, priests, religious and lay people – have an obligation to 'tradition' a truly Catholic education to the next generation. The forms of such education may require certain changes, some of them perhaps painful. Whatever the eventual outcome, the fundamental 'marks' of a Catholic ethos should remain as measures of whether or not a school is carrying out its mission according to the mind of the Church.

Without a strong system of authentically Catholic schools, the Church's mission of evangelisation in Ireland will be hindered, the preparation of informed lay Catholics will be impeded and the powerful civilising influence of Christianity on society will be diminished. Catholic schools are an integral part of the organic pastoral work of the Irish Church in the third Christian millennium.[47]

Notes

1. Cf. Mt 28:20; *Lumen gentium*, 16; Code of Canon Law, canon 794 §1.
2. John Paul II, *Ad limina* Address to Bishops of the United States, 30 May 1998, p. 2.
3. John Paul II, *Ad limina* Address to Bishops of the United States, 24 June 2004, p. 1.
4. Cf. Congregation for Catholic Education, *The Catholic School on the Threshold of the Third Millennium* (1997), p. 11. See also the excellent study by Dermot A. Lane, *Catholic Education and the School: Some Theological Reflections*, Dublin: Veritas, 1991.
5. Sacred Congregation for Catholic Education, *The Catholic School* (1977), p. 29.
6. Second Vatican Ecumenical Council, *Gravissimum educationis*, n. 8.
7. John Paul II, Address to Catholic Educators, New Orleans, 12 September 1987, p. 7.
8. N. 34.
9. Sacred Congregation for Catholic Education, *The Catholic School* (1977), p. 35.
10. R. Scott Appleby, 'Catholicism as Comprehensive Way of Life', *Origins*, 32:22 (7 November 2002), p. 370.
11. Congregation for Catholic Education, *The Catholic School on the Threshold of the Third Millennium* (1997), p. 14.
12. John Paul II, *Ad limina* Address to Bishops of the United States, 30 May 1998, p. 4.
13. Paul VI, *Evangelii nuntiandi*, n. 41.
14. Sacred Congregation for Catholic Education, *Lay Catholics in Schools: Witnesses to Faith* (1982), p. 32.
15. John Paul II, Address to the General Chapter of the Irish Christian Brothers, 22 March 2002, p. 2.
16. Cf. *The Catholic School*, 36; John Paul II, *Vita consecrata*, n. 96.
17. Cf. Congregation for Catholic Education, *The Religious Dimension of Education in a Catholic School* (1988).
18. John Paul II, *Novo millennio ineunte*, n. 43.
19. Second Vatican Ecumenical Council, *Gravissimum Educationis*, n. 3.
20. John Paul II, *Familiaris consortio*, n. 36.
21. John Paul II, *Familiaris consortio*, n. 40.
22. Second Vatican Ecumenical Council, *Gravissimum educationis*, n. 3.
23. Cf. *The Catholic School*, n. 72; Congregation for Bishops, *Directory for the Pastoral Ministry of Bishops* (2004), p. 133.
24. John Paul II, *Ad limina* Address to American Bishops, 28 October 1983, n. 7.
25. Cf. Code of Canon Law, cf. canon 375.

26 Code of Canon Law, canon 794 §1.
27 John Paul II, *Pastores gregis*, n. 52.
28 Cf. Code of Canon Law, canon 802 §1.
29 Cf. Code of Canon Law, canon 803 §1.
30 Cf. Code of Canon Law, canon 806 §1.
31 Cf. Code of Canon Law, canon 803 §2.
32 Cf. Second Vatican Ecumenical Council, *Lumen gentium*, n. 36.
33 Cf. Code of Canon Law, canon 805.
34 John Paul II, *Ad limina* Address to Bishops of the United States, 24 June 2004, n. 3.
35 Cf. John Paul II, *Pastores gregis*, n. 51.
36 Cf. John Paul II, *Ex corde ecclesiae*, n. 28.
37 John Paul II, *Vita consecrata*, n. 96.
38 Idem.
39 Second Vatican Ecumenical Council, *Christus dominus*, n. 35.
40 N. 97; cf. *The Catholic School*, p. 89; Congregation for Catholic Education, *Consecrated Persons and their Mission in Schools* (2002).
41 N. 102; cf. Code of Canon Law, canon 680.
42 *The Catholic School*, p. 71.
43 *Lay Catholics in Schools*, p. 37.
44 Second Vatican Ecumenical Council, *Apostolicam actuositatem*, n. 25.
45 Cf. *The Catholic School*, p. 70.
46 Code of Canon Law, canon 803 §2.
47 Cf. The *Catholic School on the Threshold of the Third Millennium*, p. 12.

Church, State and Education in Contemporary Ireland: Some Perspectives

John Coolahan

INTRODUCTION

This paper is organised under the following headings:

- A new era of educational change;
- Church–State relations on education pre-1922;
- Church–State relations on education 1922–1960;
- The re-shaping of State and Church in modern Ireland;
- The contemporary educational environment;
- Congruence of the educational challenge and the church mission for the new era.

The view is taken that it is only by identifying and clarifying Church–State relations on education in the past that a secure foundation can be laid for cooperative endeavour in a fast changing educational environment. A frank appraisal of the strengths and weaknesses of the Catholic Church's engagement with education in earlier times may help pave the way for an enlightened involvement of the Church in the future. Great changes have been taking place in both Church and State over recent decades in Ireland. The education system has also been altering radically in response to significant social, economic, cultural and technological change, occurring at both international and national levels. It is timely to stand back and consider some of the key issues which need to be addressed in the context of current circumstances, and new attitudes in both Church and State.

A NEW ERA OF EDUCATIONAL CHANGE

It is generally accepted that we are now living through one of those historical eras of civilisation change in which concentrated, accelerated change in many societal areas has a pervasive and fundamental impact on the configuration of society, such as happened during the Renaissance or the Industrial Revolution. The epithet of the 'knowledge society' is increasingly applied to the contemporary and emerging period. Among the characteristics of the knowledge society is the unprecedented expansion of the knowledge base across a range of disciplines. The era of globalisation with its impact on markets, manpower, capital and production is having major impacts on established modes of work and behaviour. The production of new knowledge from basic and applied research progresses in all fields of study, but most notably in science and technology. The ICT revolution is having extraordinary wide-ranging impact on communications and ways of learning, living and working. Competitiveness between firms, between nations and between trading blocs is pervasive in the pursuit of economic advantage. The structure of inherited employment patterns is undergoing major change. The globalised drive for economic growth is raising major questions on environmental sustainability. The over-exploitation of natural resources and the lack of control over greenhouse gases have raised the spectre of global warming, with potentially massive disruption to planet earth.

Many characteristics of the social changes of the era pose new challenges for the well-being of civilisation. The family, as a social institution, has been undergoing major changes in most societies, with some deleterious consequences. Many societies are becoming rapidly multi-cultural and pose new challenges for the protection of human rights, respect for the diversity of cultures and fostering social cohesion. With the increased emphasis on knowledge and the exercise of multi-faceted competencies, there is an increasing danger of a proportion of the population falling seriously behind their peers and being excluded from many of the benefits of social living. Modern society has also witnessed the inter-penetrative influences of the media and advertising, with huge impact on people's behaviour, not always of a benign nature. Young people, in particular, are increasingly exposed to destructive sub-cultures, involving drug and alcohol abuse as well as forms of sexual behaviour, giving rise to many problems.

It could be said that we are living through the best and the worst of times. The knowledge society poses many challenges for education systems. But there are also great opportunities. Before examining how the State and Church may cooperate in educational endeavour for this new era, I would like to reflect on key trends and developments in their inter-relationships in the past. The first period relates to the pre-independence era, the second is the four decades following independence and the third relates to more recent decades leading to the contemporary context. From the Church's perspective I have elsewhere taken the first period as one of winning control of education, the second as one of maintaining control and the more recent era as that of sharing control.[1] Even a brief appraisal of key characteristics of Church engagement in the periods in question can provide a helpful background on which to base reflections on future involvement. Characteristics of contemporary Irish education are examined in the later sections of this paper and surmises are made regarding the congruence between the challenges posed by this context and objectives and values of the Catholic Church.

CHURCH–STATE RELATIONS ON EDUCATION PRE-1922

Prior to the nineteenth century, the state's approach to Catholic education was hostile and could be most notably characterised by the system of penal legislation, with many prohibitions on such education. However, this did not inhibit the Catholic population from providing education for themselves and they founded what were known as the hedge or pay schools. These were schools of the people, for the people, by the people. They were much more common than is often realised. For instance, the educational census of 1824 recorded that there were over 9,300 such schools, catering for some 400,000 pupils. In the early nineteenth century, in the post Act of Union climate, the British government became activated on the Irish education situation. In 1812 a commission held that the guiding principle for state action should be, 'No attempt shall be made to influence or disturb the peculiar religious tenets of any sect or description of Christians'.[2] In the context of the time this was a progressive position in that it eschewed the policy of proselytism which had been prevalent. The new policy adopted by the state in its support of educational provision was to back the combined education of pupils of different denominations for secular subjects, allowing separate provision for denominational instruction. The national school system was inaugurated in 1831, as a state-aided system, on this basis.

The State continued with a pro-active approach to education. Educational provision in Ireland was in contrast to the ideology of *laissez faire*, so pervasive in nineteenth century Britain. A training college for male teachers was opened in Marlborough Street, Dublin in 1838, and a college for female trainee teachers in Talbot Street in 1842. These were conducted on the mixed denominational education principle. During the period 1848 to 1867 the state built twenty-seven District Model Schools which, as well as being schools, provided apprenticeship-type training for aspirants to the teaching career. As the great famine took hold in the mid-1840s the state took what was a remarkable initiative for its time – the building of three university colleges at Cork, Galway and Belfast which, in 1849, became constituent colleges of a new Queen's University.

The concept of these university colleges and the curricula offered by them were very progressive at that time, but were conceived on the mixed education principle. A commission in 1858 recommended the initiation of a state-supported intermediate (secondary) school system, also on the mixed education principle, but this did not find favour. Then, in the wake of the census of 1871 (which indicated that the Catholic proportion of the population had limited access to secondary education), the issue of state support for secondary schooling again came to the surface. A bill was drafted which included state support for secondary school buildings and the provision of a school inspectorate but, following negotiations with Catholic interests, these provisions were dropped. The ensuing Intermediate Education Act of 1878 involved a more limited role for State, confined to a payment by results role, whereby secondary schools, established by private initiative, chose to submit their pupils for state public examinations, upon the results of which payments were made to school managers. The Act was more delimited in its influence than had been intended, but it did have a significant effect on the conduct of schools, which now depended on pupils' examination results for any state financial subvention.

In 1899, the State introduced legislation for the establishment of the Department of Agriculture and Technical Instruction, which was of landmark importance for technical education in Ireland. In this instance, public funds were available on a capitation basis, in the light of inspectors' reports. Following much discussion, a resolution to the Irish university question was reached in 1908, with the Irish Universities Act. This Act established the National University of Ireland, with its three constituent colleges of University College Cork, University College Galway and University College Dublin. Shortly before independence, in 1919, the State drew up the Irish Education Bill. This was a very comprehensive, legislative measure for education in the island of Ireland, the most comprehensive attempt at education legislation for Ireland until the Education Act of 1998.

One outlines this sequence of State educational initiatives because they represent part of the historic record that tends to be overlooked. The state was quite pro-active regarding educational provision. It is sometimes implied that this was not so, and that the churches took up the running in the provision of education because of the absence of other agencies. Such a perspective does not represent the whole truth. It is true that the mixed education principle, upon which the State based most of its educational initiatives, did not recommend itself to the churches, which viewed schooling as an arena for denominational evangelisation. However, it is of some importance to note the extent and range of the State's promotion of education in that era.

The Catholic Church's reaction to the State initiatives was one of opposition to mixed education and a strengthening demand for State support for denominational education. It tolerated the national school system of 1831, but succeeded in re-shaping it to a *de facto* denominational system by the second half of the nineteenth century. A bishop's pastoral in 1900 stated:

> The system of National Education ... has itself undergone a radical change, and, in a great part of Ireland is now, in fact, whatever it is in name, as denominational almost as we could desire. In most of its schools there is no mixed education whatsoever.[3]

The national school initiative proved to be a remarkably successful one. Initially it was intended as a State-supported system for the poor but people gravitated to it and largely ignored the rows about denominationalism. By the end of the century there were over 8,000 nationals schools, attended by about 95 per cent of the school-going population. To a large extent, it was the only type of formal education for the majority of the population, and a proportion of pupils stayed on in these schools well into their teens.

In 1850, the Synod of Thurles declared strong opposition to the State's involvement in education and to mixed denominational education. It opposed the newly established Queen's University and the colleges at Cork, Galway and Belfast. The bishops established the Catholic University in 1854, in opposition to the State's initiative. In 1863 Archbishop Cullen condemned Catholic students attending the Model Schools. In 1875 he established St Patrick's Training College and in 1877 became manager of a new Sisters of Mercy Training College in Baggot Street, Dublin. These were denominational colleges for Catholic male and female student teachers, which operated as a counter to the institutions already established by the state.

In 1858, an official report urged that the State should support the provision of secondary schools, on the mixed education principle. The following year, after a meeting of Catholic Bishops in Cork, they issued the following statement:

> No form of intermediate (secondary) education is suited to a Catholic people, unless it is granted to them in separate schools, and in terms always strictly in accordance with the teaching and discipline of the Catholic Church.[4]

This view was re-iterated by Archbishop Cullen in 1867, when he stated, 'It is quite necessary that we should preserve our intermediate educational establishments ... free from all government control'.[5] It was these perspectives that led to the truncation of the Intermediate Education of 1878, referred to above, and which allowed for a form of state subvention for denominational secondary schooling, with no other involvement whatever by the State. Later on, at the turn of the twentieth century, when the State wished to replace the payment by results system with payments based on capitation and a state school inspection system, the school authorities would not agree with such a change.

Catholic Church opposition to the Education Bill of 1919–20 was bitter and sustained, eventually leading to the withdrawal of the measure in December 1920.[6] It was a wide-ranging reform measure which had strong support from teachers. From the Church's point of view, it involved ceding some controls, which had been hard won, to a new control agency and county committees. The debate on the Education Bill and its outcome cast long shadows on education in the two new states established on the island of Ireland by the partition settlement. In Northern Ireland the Bill influenced the shaping of the Education Act there in 1923. In the southern state the bitter debate was a warning to the new state that it would undertake significant educational legislation at its peril.

CHURCH–STATE RELATIONS ON EDUCATION 1922–60

What is most striking about State–Church relations regarding education during the first four decades following political independence was the extraordinary harmonious accord which occurred. The new State had a sequence of Ministers for Education who fully accepted the Catholic Church's position on education. Continuity of the balance of power which had been established – rather than any radical change – was the order of the day. On the eve of independence, in October 1921, the Catholic Primary School Managers' Association (CPSMA) declared:

> We feel confident that an Irish government established by the people for the people … will always recognise and respect the principles which must regulate and govern Catholic education. And, in view of pending changes in Irish education, we wish to assert the great fundamental

principle that the only satisfactory system of education for Catholics is one where Catholic children are taught in Catholic schools by Catholic teachers under Catholic control.[7]

The confidence of the CPSMA was well placed. While the State became very pro-active in curricular matters, particularly the promotion of the Irish language, other changes were largely of a routine character, and did not intrude on existing administrative arrangements. As regards secondary schooling, the first annual report of the new Department of Education for the year 1924–25 stated:

The State at present inspects these schools regularly and exercises a certain amount of supervision through its powers to make grants to schools as a result of these inspections, but it neither funds secondary schools, nor finances the building of them, nor appoints teachers or managers, nor exercises any power or veto over the appointment or dismissal of such teachers or the management of schools.[8]

This delimited role of the State was to continue for four decades. The State was making it clear that as a new State it saw no role for itself in the provision of secondary schools. It was prepared to let the Church carry the burden, which it was quite willing to do, as it would both own and control the secondary schools.

The State did make an intrusion in the area of technical education. In 1930 the Vocational Education Act was passed, setting out an updated framework for continuation and technical schools, under local authority control. Significantly, however, this was only achieved following secret negotiations with the Catholic bishops, in which the Minister for Education gave guarantees that the vocational schools would not engage in liberal or humane studies and would be confined to practical and applied subjects.[9]

So, in 1931, Professor Corcoran SJ, Professor of Education in UCD, and a very influential figure in educational circles at the time, could report to a conference of Catholic educators in Belgium that:

> The Catholic ownership of Catholic primary schools is secured in nearly all cases, and the Catholic character of all subjects of instruction is guaranteed by the presence of Catholic teachers, using books acceptable to Catholics … The Catholic secondary schools are always the property of the pastoral clergy and of Religious Orders of men and women, only some six small schools are controlled by Catholic lay teachers.[10]

This statement represented the institutional type of thinking that prevailed at the time. Very little, if any, public unease was expressed about such arrangements for schooling. A high degree of stability prevailed, with no radical re-thinking about the role of education taking place. Successive governments did not differ on educational policy.

John Whyte, in *Church and State in Modern Ireland*, characterised State–Church relations in this period as follows:

> Over most of the period since independence, the remarkable feature of educational policy in Ireland has been the reluctance of the State to touch on the entrenched positions of the Church. This is not because the Church's claims have been moderate; on the contrary, it has carved out for itself a more extensive control over education in Ireland than in any other country in the world. It is because the Church has insisted on its claims with such force that the State has been extremely cautious in entering its domain.[11]

To achieve this position in education required a very great deal of effort by Church personnel. It needed a great deal of time, ingenuity, resources, commitment and endeavour on the part of many such personnel to achieve such an impressive schooling framework. Many of those involved – and their successors – are justifiably proud of this achievement. Yet, it is striking that many historians and social scientists who have written on the history of Irish education at that time tend to be quite critical rather than praising in their evaluations. Thus, authors such as Akenson, Atkinson, Titley, O'Donoghue, McElligott, Ó Buachalla, Farren, Fitzgerald, Whyte, Fuller, Lynch and Garvin raise questions about the nature and value of the educational control exercised by Catholic Church agencies in these decades.

At this time of reflection regarding new directions for a changing contemporary educational environment, it is worth considering why this might be so. There was a very strong concentration on issues such as control, ownership, patronage, trusteeship, appointments, dismissals and exclusivity. There was a great reliance on legal rights to maintain control. A tradition of top-down decision making tended to prevail. A very limited role was conceded to the laity, particularly in secondary schools. Attitudes to the curriculum were conservative and complacent. The style of pedagogy was mainly teacher-centred and didactic. The rights of parents were formally conceded, but parents were kept at a considerable remove from the education process. Schools tended to be very self-contained with little or no contact with their supportive communities. Isolation from the public affairs external to the school was regarded as a particular virtue in boarding schools. An obstructive spirit towards reforms could be in evidence. Despite the remarkably benign attitude of the State, suspicions of the state in relation to education was never far from the surface. Dermot Lane would see such attitudes as rooted in the Counter-Reformation Church, which still existed at the time and which was 'defensive, exclusivist and introverted'.[12]

While such characteristics need to be evaluated in the context of the times which prevailed, they have left a residue of perspectives which ought to be acknowledged. There may also be useful lessons to be drawn.

Of course, there were admirable characteristics in evidence which it is also important to acknowledge. These would include the remarkable commitment, dedication and unselfishness of so many Church personnel as they carried out their educational work. The religious values which they promoted through their work were of great importance. The investment of fiscal resources in educational infrastructure was an important contribution, particularly in the context of the State's parsimoniousness with expenditure for education. Many of the clergy provided good quality educational leadership and ran their schools efficiently and effectively. Most Church personnel exhibited high integrity in their lifestyles and relationships. The schools contributed significantly to the high levels of educational achievement attained by a minority of the population in those decades. Because of their position in society, Church personnel conferred social status on the teaching career, which became the life's work of so many men and women in the clerical and religious life.

THE RE-SHAPING OF STATE AND CHURCH IN MODERN IRELAND

The post-1960 period involved an era of extensive and accelerated social, economic, political and cultural change which was to be a prelude to the Celtic Tiger era of the 1990s and the impact of the knowledge society. The state assumed a more active role in educational policy in structural, curricular and managerial areas. While in the 1950s Minister Mulcahy characterised the role of Minister for Education as the dungaree man who knocked the pipes to keep the system running, Minister Hillary, in the early 1960s, used the more apt metaphor of being captain of the ship. As might be expected, the new, more pro-active stance of the State regarding educational policy and practice gave rise to instances of tension with church interests. In a celebrated article in the publication *Studies*, in autumn 1968, Mr Seán O Connor, Assistant Secretary of the Department of Education, referred to the situation in the following manner:

> I lay stress on these things because I believe a change must be made, otherwise there will be an explosion, maybe sooner than later. No one wants to push the religious out of education; that would be disastrous, in my opinion. But I want them in as partners, not always as masters. I believe that there is need for dialogue at the highest level between Church and State on the problems in education now surfacing ... The dialogue must be frank and range over a wide area.[13]

The explosion did not occur, but a great deal of dialogue took place. Despite surface difficulties, the Catholic bishops displayed adroit leadership in coming to terms with new educational developments. One of the significant developments was the introduction of two new types of post-primary school – the comprehensive school and the community school. Seamus Ó Buachalla in *Education in Twentieth Century Ireland* formed the view:

> Perhaps the major contribution of the Catholic bishops to policy in that decade [1960s] lay not only in shaping the nature of the proposals coming forward, but in securing their acceptance of the government policies by the Catholic managerial bodies, in the creation of an effective consultative infrastructure and in influencing the character of the comprehensive and community schools so that they approximated, as closely as possible, to the Catholic ideal in management, ownership and staffing.[14]

Thus, despite hysterical charges by some religious interests that the State was 'nationalising education by stealth',[15] a new *modus vivendi* evolved between Church and State on the modernising of education.

While the State was re-shaping itself and galvanising itself in the context of significant societal change, the same was happening in the case of the other partner, the Catholic Church. The Vatican II Council of the early 1960s was a landmark event in the history of Catholicism and was to have profound effects on the Catholic Church in Ireland. From the early 1970s a decline in vocations to the religious life became apparent, a decline which has continued its very steep fall up to the present. It was also the case that greater numbers left the religious life and became laicised. The impact of the Church as an authoritative voice began to wane. In the changed circumstances of the 1980s and 1990s many of the religious congregation engaged in an in-depth reflection on their role in relation to their original charism. The nature of their involvement in education came under fresh scrutiny. As they looked back at their historical experience the question was raised as to whether they might have created a trap for themselves by such a close, cosy relationship with the State, following independence. A publication of the Conference of Religious in Ireland put the matter in the following way:

> The early efforts of religious congregations were so successful that they had by the 1880s become part of a new establishment. As Corish (1985) suggests, the Catholic Church become a 'kind of semi-state body'. Being part of a new establishment, particularly when the Catholic nation achieved state power, entailed a dramatic change in the *raison d'être* of religious in education. No longer were they running schools which were in some way counter-cultural; instead, their schools were now some of the principal *agents of socialisation* [original

emphasis] into the values and outlook of the new establishment.[16]

The churches from the mid-1970s, with State encouragement, moved to adopt a partnership approach with parents and teachers in the management of schools. With the decline in religious personnel, lay principals were appointed to many schools. New forms of trusteeship have been evolved by many religious congregations whereby their educational aims may be promoted in very changed circumstances from those which prevailed in the past. Efforts have been made to engage in strategic planning and consolidation of effort. Targeted educational interventions have been devised along the lines of the congregations' charism. A great deal of constructive work has been undertaken which should prove of great value in the years ahead. As the new century opens up, Irish society is wealthier, more materialistic, secular, pluralist and multi-ethnic than it had been during the nineteenth and twentieth centuries. This dynamically changed society requires different educational responses from those which hitherto operated.

THE CONTEMPORARY EDUCATIONAL ENVIRONMENT

Since the early 1990s Irish education has been undergoing a period of impressive reform and development. This process of policy making was distinguished by the highly consultative approach taken with all the stakeholders. Events such as the National Education Convention (1993) and the National Forum on Early Childhood Education (1998) were important instances of the consultative approach being taken. Two Green Papers and three White Papers were published on different aspects of education. A raft of educational legislation was enacted. While some tension existed in Church–State relations on issues such as school management, the view expressed by Bishop Flynn at a conference of the future management of schools, in 1994, was not representative of general attitudes:

> We find within the documents on the governance of
> schools and on the Regional Education Councils the
> bricks of a secularist agenda and a bid to control the
> schools to such an extent as to undermine the principle of
> subsidiarity. The ideology behind some of these
> proposals is seen by some bishops as an attempt by the
> State to push the Church out of education.[17]

In fact, the constructive character of Church–State relationships
was reflected in the Education Act of 1998, a fact which has
been acknowledged by Church personnel. The State investment
in education has increased impressively from €1.5 billion in 1990
to over €7 billion in 2005. Ireland has now achieved what is
known as 'the schooled society'. Over 80 per cent of young
people now complete post-primary schooling, while another
minority engage in alternative education and training
programmes such as Youthreach and community training
workshops. Of the cohort of school leavers, 60 per cent go into
some form of tertiary education. A generation ago the
proportion was only about 5 per cent. We are now moving from
the schooled society to the 'learning society', in the context of
the policy of lifelong learning, which has been adopted by the
government. Along with the traditional three tiers of the
mainstream education system – primary, post-primary and
tertiary education – White Papers have been issued on early
childhood education and on adult learning. A cradle to grave
approach to education is now official policy.

The role of the school, inherited from industrial society, is
being re-conceptualised in line with the needs of the knowledge
society. Within the re-conceptualisation more emphasis is being
placed on the school as a living and learning community, rather
than as a series of education units behind classroom doors. The
school is also being seen as having more permeable

relationships with its external community. Links with the external world of work and with local community activities are being fostered. It is also policy now to establish the school as an 'inclusive' community wherein all pupils are accommodated, regardless of ability levels.

Partnership in school management between trustees, parents, teachers and the local community is now well established, even if it does not always operate to its optimal level. A bottom-up approach to internal planning operates in schools which emphasises the importance of collaboration and collegiality between all the involved parties. This allows schools to mark out their own vision, to put their individual stamp on their endeavours and to prioritise issues suited to their needs and environments. School ethos is promoted as dynamic, organic development, not as something which is handed down. By concretising it and by rooting it in the community life of the school it avoids the danger, to which Archbishop Martin has drawn attention, of becoming 'an ethereal concept'. School mission statements are intended to animate the school planning process. They incorporate the values and overall aims of the school. What is crucial is that they do not become pious statements for public relations occasions, but that they are seen to be lived-out in the relationships and way of life of the school. It is important for staff and students to feel that such statements have a real influence on their lives within the school.

The policy commitment in Irish education is towards holistic education. It seems to me that when one examines relevant Vatican II documents on education there is a great concordance between them and what Irish education seeks to develop. Curriculum is a rolling reform issue in our schools. The Primary School Curriculum of 1999, whose implementation is now being rolled out, is one of the most progressive curricula in the modern world. It sets out an impressive conception of child nature, places the child's dignity within a balanced educational process and offers a very comprehensive range of educational experiences. The post-primary curricula have been undergoing massive change, including the incorporation of Transition Year, Leaving Certificate Applied, Leaving Certificate Vocational programmes, allied to a reform 'established' Leaving Certificate Programme. The NCCA has recently issued a major consultative paper directed towards key reforms in senior cycle. The proposals are creative and imaginative and hold out much promise if they are implemented. Religion continues to be a taught subject in schools, but its status has been enhanced by the introduction of an examination-based programme, with State support. It is a very enlightened, exciting and challenging programme.

In the context of a lifelong learning policy, the 'learning to learn' motif is moving centre-stage in the education process. The aim is to equip pupils with the competencies, confidence and motivation to go on learning, encouraging more self-reliance and less dependency among pupils. The balance between teaching and learning is shifting, with much more emphasis now being placed on the learning process. The incorporation of ICT into the teaching and learning process is also being urged in contemporary schooling. Special attention is being given to the needs of weak learners. Something of a revolution has taken place in this regard, with the recruitment of about 5,000 learning support teachers in primary schools.

Much emphasis is being placed on the quality of relationships within schools. This is rather well expressed in Chapter 13 of the White Paper, *Charting Our Education Future*. The role of guidance counselling and pastoral care is also receiving more attention and is benefiting from more professionally skilled people in schools. This is particularly important for today's teenagers who are exposed to so many countervailing values to those being promoted by the home and the school. The provision of home/school/community liaison personnel in many schools, particularly in disadvantaged areas, builds bridges between school personnel, parents and community interests. This scheme has been recognised by the OECD as being distinctive and very beneficial.

Congruence between the Challenges of Contemporary Education and the Catholic Church's Education Mission?

I consider that the circumstances of the contemporary Irish educational environment provide an arena for – as well as suggest an agenda for – the Church's education mission, both within and outside the school. The characteristics being sought of educators are of a high order – imaginative, creative, innovative, empathic, caring people with collegial skills and capable of divergent thinking, questioning, coping with uncertainty, risk taking and guided by strong ethical values. These are different qualities than would have been emphasised in earlier times. However, I believe they are congruent with both the spirit and the letter of the renewal of Church thinking on education as represented in Vatican II documents. Rather than inculcation and docile receptivity of pupils, the learning process now encourages more interaction and a questioning approach from pupils to allow for genuine personalisation of the subject matter. In the more secular society of today there is a sharper realisation of the centrality of beliefs and values as a basis for moral action. It is ironic that what could sometimes be a rather unthinking, taking for granted response to religious content and values in a more stable type of society is being replaced by an appetite for and more engaged interest in such material during an era of uncertainty and accelerated change. It is significant that much new thinking from religious personnel embraces this contemporary challenge with confidence and a sense of purpose, seeing education as a process of transformation. As instances, I would mention Sean Healy and Brigid Reynold's publication, *Irish Society and the Future of Education* (2000) and CORI's *Religious Congregations in Irish Education: A Role for the Future* (2001).

It is desirable that the Church personnel give sustained attention to educational policy trends and engage in policy analysis. This relates to international groups such as the EU and the OECD as to national developments. A good 'reading' of statistical patterns can help in the prioritisation of manpower in relation to mission. The scope for greater networking between institutions and between agencies can give much added value to efforts. The establishment by many religious congregations of education offices with specialist personnel in support of front-line education effort is a very creditable development. Such support services allow for capacity building. The building of alliances between cognate parties maximises impact. The role of NGOs in association with other partners in social partnership agreements has helped to target more resources for education and for vulnerable groups with regard to education.

In a more multi-cultural, multi-ethnic society there is a need for more diverse types of school. It is in the interests of Catholic education that more school choice is available. As Dermot Lane has written:

> The Catholic Church, therefore, should welcome the development of other alternative forms of educational choice such as Gaelscoileanna, multi-denominational education and non-denominational education ... such diversity of form and choice in education can only be good for Catholic education as it will act as a stimulus to develop what is distinctive about its own identity and ethos. The absence of diversity in education in the past has not always served the best interests of Catholic education.[18]

There will be some denominational schools with multi-denominational pupils and, perhaps, non-believing pupils. Vatican II admits the need for active engagement with inter-faith dialogue in schools as in society at large, with respect being shown to non-Christian belief systems. As Archbishop Martin remarked, 'Religious education should be understood as an exciting project, which is truly in harmony with a modern pluralist society'.

A distinguishing feature of the work of many Catholic educators in the past was their commitment to the education of the poor and the marginalised. Despite the greatly increased wealth generated by the Celtic Tiger, the incidence of poverty continues to be a harsh reality for a large minority of the population. It may well be that the gap is widening between those who 'have' and 'can do' and those who 'have not' and 'can't do'. Social inclusion is an EU and a national goal but, as Combat Poverty and other agencies such as the Vincent de Paul Society regularly remind us, poverty is a persistent reality, blighting the lives of many. The tremendous contribution of Catholic educators to the underprivileged continues to be needed and the regeneration of charisms has re-emphasised the importance of a preferential option for the poor, in education as in other areas.

The teaching of religion as a subject requires the highest levels of pedagogic competence. While very significant progress has been made in the formation of religious educators, the issue should not be taken for granted and it requires serious attention. There needs to be a review of the situation which would identify the strengths and weaknesses of current provision, with a view to taking action on the latter. In-career development at both primary and post-primary teacher levels would merit particular attention.

With declining numbers of Catholic clergy and religious, it is essential to engage the wide scale involvement of lay Catholics. Vatican II gave a special emphasis to the role of the laity within the Church. At present, there is a remarkable popularity for courses in religious studies, of tertiary education level, throughout the country. This is a phenomenon which needs to be harnessed in the general interest of Catholic education. This is linked to the engagement of parents, who have the primary responsibility for the education of their children, to take their duties seriously in religious formation. In contemporary society this tends to be more easily said than done, but progress is being made in many areas. Adult catechesis has not been strong in the Irish tradition. There are promising signs that this situation is improving, in a lifelong learning era. Dermot Lane draws attention to such developments and the need for the Catholic school to have bridgeheads on to its supportive community. He states:

> In recent years Catholic schools have been building bridges between the school, the parish and the home in all kinds of different ways: parenting programmes, school-parish projects, bridge-building between school catechesis and parish catechesis. These initiatives and others must continue to be developed and expanded. The concept of the Catholic school in isolation is a contradiction in terms.[19]

There is a striking confidence in how CORI sees its role for the future when it identifies it as one of 'Trailblazing, Advocacy and Alliances'. One cannot but admire the conviction behind such a motto for action. The confidence of bearing Christian witness at a time when some consider that the 'centre cannot hold' is very important for the Catholic Church and for the well-being of society at large. We are not just passive victims in a new societal era, we also have the privilege of helping to shape that era. Christian witness ought to be a central shaping agency, as there is a great deal at stake. When one examines the contemporary educational environment one finds much that is integral to the values of Catholic education and much that can be improved by a renewed Christian witness in relation to the emerging challenges. The three cardinal virtues of faith, hope and love are highly pertinent to the education process and, in this case, I suggest that the most important of them for us is hope.

Notes

1   John Coolahan, 'Church–State Relations in Primary and Secondary Education' in James P. Mackey and Enda McDonagh (eds) *Religion and Politics in Ireland at the Turn of the Millennium*, Dublin: Columba Press, 2003, pp. 132–51.

2   John Coolahan, *Irish Education: History and Structure*, Dublin: Institute of Public Administration, 2002 edn, p. 10.

3   Pastoral quoted in *The Irish Teachers' Journal*, 6 October 1900, p. 4

4   E.R. Norman, *The Catholic Church and Ireland in the Age of Rebellion, 1859–73*, London: Longmans, 1965, p. 59.

5   Quoted by Alfred O'Rahilly, 'The Irish University Question VII – Secondary Education', *Studies*, L1, 1962, pp. 147–55.

6   John Coolahan, 'The Education Bill of 1919–20: Problems of Educational Reform', *Proceedings of the Educational Studies Association of Ireland*, 1979, pp. 11–31.

7   Reported in *The Times Educational Supplement*, 22 October 1921, p. 323.

8   *Report of the Department of Education for 1924–25*, Dublin: Stationary Office, 1925, p. 7.

9   Letter from J.M. O'Sullivan, Minister for Education, to the Most Rev. Dr Keane, Bishop of Limerick, 31 October 1930.

10 Rev. T. Corcoran, *The Catholic Schools of Ireland*, Louvain, 1931, p. 6.

11 John H. Whyte, *Church and State in Modern Ireland, 1923–70*, Dublin: Gill & Macmillan, 1971, p. 21.

12 Dermot A. Lane, 'The Expanding Horizons of Catholic Education' in Padraig Hogan and Kevin Williams (eds) *The Future of Religion in Irish Education*, Dublin: Veritas, 1993, pp. 128–38, 130.

13 Sean O'Connor, 'Post-Primary Education: Now and in the Future', *Studies*, Autumn 1968, Vol. L VII, pp. 233–49.

14 Seamus Ó Buachalla, *Education Policy in Twentieth Century Ireland*, Dublin: Wolfhound, 1988, pp. 232/233.

15 Teaching Brothers' Association, 'Comment on Sean O'Connor's Article', *Studies*, 1968, pp. 274–83.

16 Conference of the Religious in Ireland (CORI), *Religious Congregations in Irish Education: A Role for the Future*, Dublin: CORI, 1997, p. 15.

17 Quoted in John Walshe, *A New Partnership in Education*, Dublin: Institute of Public Administration, 1999, p. 107.

18 Dermot A. Lane, op. cit, p. 137.

19 Dermot A. Lane, *Catholic Education and the School: Some Theological Reflections*, Dublin: Veritas, 1991, p. 18.

Challenges Facing Catholic Education in Ireland

Dermot A. Lane

INTRODUCTION

I am grateful to the organisers for the opportunity to present a paper to this tripartite conference. In a sense I am an outsider to the proceedings – being neither a religious nor a bishop nor a member of a Roman congregation. This puts me in a privileged position of being able to criticise all three!

The way we perceive the challenge facing Catholic education will influence the way we approach the issue. Let me begin, therefore, by offering three different quotations which summarise what I see as the challenge facing Catholic education today and at the same time capture succinctly the spirit of much of what I want to say in this paper:

The first quotation is from Jacques Delors:

In these times of intense change, nothing is more difficult than discovering what should change and what should remain constant. Only education can mediate between the tendency either to rely exclusively on what is new or on its opposite, a conservatism that tends to turn entirely towards the past. Education alone has the ability to pass on to students what humanity has learned about itself while at the same time providing the tools that allow everyone to face a future that is both new and uncertain.[1]

111

Note how Delors emphasises education as a process of passing on what humanity has learned about itself. It is a central conviction of Catholic education that humanity learned something decisive about itself in the story of Jesus of Nazareth, crucified and risen. Catholic education, therefore, is committed to keeping the disturbing, liberating and healing memory of Jesus alive in our world. Memory is a key element in Catholic education.

My second quotation comes from Mary Warnock:

> I have ... come very strongly to believe that it is the cultivation of imagination which should be the chief aim of education ... We have a duty to educate the imagination above all else ... So imagination ... is necessary ... if we are to see the world as significant of something unfamiliar, if we are ever to treat the objects of perception as symbolising ... things other than themselves.[2]

Part of the failure in Catholic education today is a crisis of the imagination. For too many, Catholic education has become stuck in a pre-Vatican II configuration of the religious imagination. Putting together these two quotations we come up with a view of Catholic education as a process of effecting a creative unity between memory and imagination, a critical correlation between the liberating memory of Jesus Christ as the Wisdom of God and the imaginative insertion of that subversive memory into the understanding of the world today.

It took the genius of Patrick Kavanagh to point out that 'On the stem of memory, creative imaginations flourish'.[3] Something similar is found in Augustine in his *Confessions* where he emphasises the unity of memory and imagination in coming to know the self and God. I want to suggest even at this early stage in my paper that memory and imagination are key elements in any reconfiguration of Catholic education for the third millennium.

My third quotation is taken from the Second Vatican Council which says 'the Church always has the duty of scrutinising the signs of the times and of interpreting them in the light of the Gospel'.[4] It is only when the Church seeks to acknowledge and understand the complexity of the world in which it exists that it can become a significant player in education. It is not enough, in this era of exploding new knowledge, simply to repeat the past in the present; instead the vitality of Catholic education is found in its capacity to effect a transformation of the present through the prophetic, creative and redemptive elements of the Good News of Jesus, crucified and risen, and now active through the Spirit of Christ in the church and the world.

There have been significant developments in Irish education in the last ten years and these are part of the context in which the challenges facing Catholic education should be understood. On the side of the State, these developments include:

- Universities Act, 1997;
- Education Act, 1998;
- Education Welfare Act, 2000;
- White Paper on Adult Education, 2001;
- Report for the OECD by Professor John Coolahan on 'Attracting Developing and Retraining Effective Teachers', 2003;
- Education for People with Special Education Needs, 2004;
- OECD Report on Higher Education, 2004.

Alongside these documents there has been the establishment of the National Association of Principals and Vice Principals of Secondary Schools (1998), the coming into being of Irish Primary Principals Network (2000), the establishment of the National Framework of Qualifications (2004) and the setting up of a new Teacher Council (2005). These developments are to be welcomed and are changing for the better the landscape of Irish education.

On the Church side the following is a sample of important documents:

- *General Directory for Catechesis*, Congregation for the Clergy, 1997;
- *Guidelines for the Faith Formation and Development of Catholic Students*, Irish Bishops, 1999;
- *Consecrated Persons and their Mission in Schools*, Congregation for Catholic Education, 2002;
- *The Catholic School on the Threshold of the Third Millennium*, 2002;
- A working paper entitled, *Towards a Policy for RE in Post-Primary Schools*, 2004;
- *Be Good News*, Draft National Directory for Catechesis, Irish Bishops' Conference, 2006.

These documents in turn have been followed by the establishment by the bishops of a new National Catechetical Office and the appointment of a full-time director to that office, the loosely constituted Education Consultative Group, and a new appointment to the CORI Education Desk (2002).

I mention these developments simply to highlight the fact that while there has been progress on both sides, insufficient attention has been given to these two streams in public debate about education. It is as if these developments in Church and State run on parallel tracks without any serious engagement between what is happening in secular education and Catholic education. The convening of this Conference is a unique opportunity to initiate a more critical but constructive conversation between secular education and Catholic education.

In the above context I would like to try to do three things in this paper:

1 Describe some recent developments in education;
2 Analyse some cultural shifts that challenge Catholic education;
3 Offer some concrete proposals.

PART 1: A DESCRIPTION OF DEVELOPMENTS IN EDUCATION

Primary Schools

There is an ever-increasing awareness and appreciation of the importance of primary school education as that which influences and determines the future of a young person's life. Consequently this is a time for increasing local support of the good work performed by teachers in Catholic primary schools and not, therefore, a time for reducing or withdrawing that support.

As we know, the majority of primary schools in Ireland are Catholic. In recent times, however, other modes or types of primary education have developed, variously and confusingly described as multi-denominational education, inter-denominational education, non-denominational education, Gaelscoileanna and the movement known as Educate Together.

As the majority stakeholder in primary education, the Catholic Church should encourage other forms of educational provision to meet the needs of an ever-increasing pluralist, multi-cultural and secularist Ireland. At present, close collaboration takes place between the CPSMA, the Church of Ireland and the Islamic foundation as agencies of faith-based schools and this is to be welcomed. Other networks of secular education should also be developed. As we know majorities, like monopolies, have a habit of becoming complacent.

Primary education has become a flashpoint in public debate. An example of this can be found in what has become known as the Dunboyne dispute (2002) in Scoil Thulach na nÓg which created enormous media attention and gave rise to a considerable amount of misrepresentation *vis-à-vis* the nature of Catholic education and sacramental preparation. This in turn resulted in an INTO survey of teachers and a report with interesting results.[5] A more recent example of public debate was occasioned by the publication of the Ferns Report (2005) on sexual abuse. This gave rise to a campaign by a few commenatators to wrest all control of primary schools from the Catholic Church. A third example of public debate about primary schools was sparked by an article in a national newspaper by the Director of the Irish Primary Principals Network (2006). This article sought to open a debate about 'the relationship between organised religion and primary education … the provision of a proper chaplaincy service … [and] a new model of shared responsibility'. The front-page headline in the same newspaper came out as 'Heads want Communion lessons to be ditched'!

It should be noted that the INTO survey of teachers found that the majority are happy to teach religion in primary schools. However, a growing number of teachers in primary schools are, understandably, unhappy about the amount of time given over to sacramental preparation and the lack of pastoral support from parishes in the preparation of children for First Confession, First Communion and Confirmation.

Over the last number of years there has been a gradual decline of the involvement by parishes in the support of primary schools. Expressions of this decline can be found in the absence of a priest on the board of management, a reduction in the chaplaincy service and a disappearing presence of parish to the school. This loosening of links between parish and primary schools has become acute in the areas of sacramental preparation.

This decline, however, is symptomatic of a deeper problem, namely the changing character of the staffing, management and self-understanding of parishes. As is well known, parishes today, in the light of the declining number of priests, are in need of reform, renewal and reconstruction in terms of personnel, mission and vision – something that Archbishop Diarmuid Martin has begun to address in Dublin by mandating the establishment of Parish Pastoral Councils (2004), and similar moves have been taken also in other dioceses.

There are urgent issues to be addressed for the renewal of parishes in relation to lay ministry, faith formation, adult religious education and chaplaincy services – issues that I will return to later in this paper. Suffice it to note at this stage that movement on one or other of these later areas would be of enormous support to the work of teachers in Catholic primary schools.

In spite of this growing gap between parishes and national schools, there is a very successful religious education programme in existence. This programme, entitled *Alive O 1–8*, has been very well received by schools, teachers, pupils and parents, not only in Ireland but also in the UK, US, Australia, South Africa, the Diplomatic Core in the Middle East and more recently in France. This highly respected religious education programme, however, will not succeed without the support of parishes and parents.

It is unreasonable to expect Catholic teachers to take on responsibility for faith formation and sacramental preparation of pupils in primary schools without support from parishes. Further, this problem is often compounded by the absence of support from parents. At present the three agencies of Catholic education, namely the school, the parish and the home, are in danger of continuing to exist as 'islands apart' (M. Kennedy). This is one of the urgent challenges facing Catholic education today.

Second-Level Voluntary Schools

The most significant development in second-level schools has been the introduction of a new State syllabus in religious education at both Junior Certificate and Leaving Certificate levels and both syllabi are now on offer for public examination.

This development has given new life and credibility to religious education in second-level schools and this has happened at a time when religious education was not exactly distinguishing itself within the curriculum. The content and structure of these new syllabi, drawn up by the National Council for Curriculum and Assessment after wide consultation, have been well received by teachers and schools. Students are required to have a knowledge and understanding not only of Christianity but also of other religions. These syllabi are ecumenical and educationally committed to inter-religious dialogue within a multi-cultural society.

Religious education in the light of this development has now acquired a new status within the school curriculum in terms of timetable, content, standards and assessment. At Junior Certificate level most pupils take religious education as a subject for public examination. At Leaving Certificate, which is only just beginning, a small number of schools opted to take religious education for public examination in 2005. For those who do not take RE in the Leaving Certificate, the Department of Education and Science has put in place, via the NCCA, a *Framework for Senior Cycle Religious Education*. This, as the title implies, is a framework and not a syllabus in the strict sense and therefore leaves space for local planning, implementation and assessment appropriate to the school ethos over a period of two or three years.

These recent developments in religious education at second level have resulted in the following gains:

- The existence of a State-sponsored *Religious Education Support Service*;
- A pilot system of in-service for schools introducing RE for examination;
- Guidelines from the bishops concerning faith formation;
- A series of new textbooks, guidelines and resources for Junior Certificate and Leaving Certificate religious education, and for Senior Cycle religious education;

- A discussion document entitled *Towards a Policy for RE in Post-Primary Schools.*

These positive developments, however, require a certain readjustment by voluntary Catholic schools to the demands of the new State religious education syllabus. There is a need, for example, for a closer correlation between school ethos and the content of the new, State religious education programme and it should be noted that there is scope for this critical conversation to take place within the syllabus itself. In addition, there is a need for new support structures within voluntary secondary schools to augment the new religious education programme in terms of providing prayer services, focusing attention on social justice issues, initiating practical projects related to local needs and the provision of pastoral care. These developments, however, will be of little value, unless, to quote Sr Eileen Randles from another context, there is a convergence between the stated ethos of the Catholic school and the actual experience of pupils, teachers and parents.[6]

This challenge of ensuring that the school ethos is alive brings me to my second point concerning secondary voluntary schools, namely chaplaincy. Over the last five years attempts have been made to get State recognition and payment for chaplains in voluntary secondary schools in Ireland. The outcome has been one of failure by the Churches and by the State. Both Church and State have failed to provide chaplaincy support to students and staff in voluntary secondary schools at a time when we have heard so much public disquiet about increased levels of substance abuse, binge drinking, teenage pregnancy, bullying, obesity, changing social mores and suicide among young students in second-level schools.

There is more than just anecdotal evidence of the need for pastoral care and a professional chaplaincy service in voluntary secondary schools. For example, a study of 1,000 students attending second-level schools, reported in the *Irish Journal of Medical Science* (February 2006), has found that 20 per cent of pupils had significant levels of depression and that the increasing rate of marital breakdown has serious implications for the mental health of adolescents in schools.[7] Marie Cassidy, noted journalist and psychologist, writing about the tragic death of a mother and her two sons, points out that one of the most reassuring rituals in the lives of children in times of tragedy and trauma is that of prayer.[8]

Further, a survey of over 1,000 teachers conducted by the Teachers Union of Ireland (2006) has found that 20 per cent of teachers were threatened or intimidated by students, that 21 per cent of teachers witnessed physical violence by students on another pupil, that 50 per cent of teachers reported bullying of students by classmates, that 63 per cent of teachers were at the receiving end of unacceptable impertinence and defiance by students.[9]

The amendment of Section 29 of the Education Act by the Minister of Education is a welcome move in response to this survey and this will certainly help to balance the rights of individual students with the rights of students as members of a learning community within the context of the appeals process.

However, the challenges facing voluntary secondary schools in this particular pastoral context are greater than simply balancing rights within the appeals process. These findings about student behaviour are related to the growing reality of substance abuse, binge drinking and difficulties associated with sexual development among students in second-level schools. The presence of such anti-social behaviour within the school situation raises questions about the underlying sources and causes of such behaviour. Often, the causes exist outside school in terms of socio-economic factors in the home and/or peer pressure from within the local community. The issues are complex and are not easily resolved: they will require a holistic approach, embracing the inter-personal, psychological and spiritual aspects of human behaviour. Within this holistic approach, chaplains have an important role to play alongside others.

All of the high-sounding mission statements in voluntary schools and the lofty aspirations of the Education Act, 1998 and the Welfare Act of 2000 have fallen flat in the face of this inability by the Churches and the State to provide a chaplaincy service for voluntary secondary schools in Ireland. It is worth noting in passing that the Education Act, 1998 requires schools to 'promote the moral, spiritual, social and personal development of students' (sec. 9).

Coupled with this failure is the equally disturbing question of justice in terms of an educational system that provides a chaplaincy service for the VEC, community and comprehensive sector and not in the voluntary sector. To the outside observer it appears that the State is refusing to address a fundamental issue of equalisation between the voluntary sector and the VEC/community and comprehensive sectors, especially in relation to chaplaincy services. Oddly and ironically there is often better provision for religious education and chaplaincy in the State-run VEC/community sector than there is in the voluntary sector.

A further issue of justice relates to chaplains, lay and ordained, who have worked in VEC/community schools without any assurances of permanency and pension provision, not to mention those chaplains who have worked in voluntary secondary schools for non-professional salaries in *ad hoc* arrangements.

There is now an abundance of evidence through surveys that the teen years in Ireland have become more turbulent and traumatic for a variety of reasons: the changing sociology of family life, a decline in moral values and the existence of a new culture of experimentation and instant gratification.

Of course these pastoral issues are a matter of concern for all teachers within school community – but what is everybody's responsibility runs the risk of becoming nobody's responsibility.

Thus, the appointment and payment of chaplains or of coordinators of chaplaincy services within voluntary second schools is an urgent issue, needing immediate attention. The role and terms of reference for the appointment of coordinators of chaplaincy services are readily available – but is the will there to address this urgent pastoral issue in voluntary secondary schools?

Higher Education
When it comes to third-level education in Ireland it is extremely difficult to paint an accurate picture. On the one hand, more and more people are participating in third-level education – estimated by some to be 65 per cent of school leavers. On the other hand, there is little evidence of any comparable educational progress in relation to the faith development of adults in parishes. Indeed for too many adults, faith development stopped at the end of secondary schooling. Furthermore, it should be noted that most third-level education takes place in a secular context without much reference to faith, theology and church. This means, in effect, that a tension can exist between the sophistication of what graduates of universities and institutes of technology receive on the one hand and the inert state of personal faith development among graduates in parishes on the other hand. There is a serious gap between professional education and personal faith development and this in turn is aggravated by the absence of any agreed Church policy on evangelisation, adult faith formation and adult religious education within parishes.

In contrast to this situation it must be noted that some twenty-six different institutions offer some form of third-level theological and religious education. There has never been so many lay women and men in the history of Irish Catholicism studying theology in one form or another. For some reason, however, this study of theology and religious education does not seem to flow back into the building up of Christian communities at the local level. The reasons for this are difficult to unravel. They include, however, the fact that there is no career path in parishes for those who feel called to lay ministry. Another possible reason is that some of the centres often lack the inter-disciplinary challenges coming from non-theological subjects such as the humanities and the hard sciences that raise important questions about the relationship between ethics and economics, religion and science, morality and the marketplace. A further factor is the absence of serious research within many of these institutions of theology, largely because most of the centres of theology are struggling to survive and therefore depend in large measure on their capacity to increase the number of undergraduate students in order to create streams of income. This situation cries out for strategic planning regarding resources and institutional collaboration, for some degree of rationalisation and some redistribution of resources with a view to promoting greater specialisation and serious theological research in the Irish context.

The Churches in Ireland need theology more than ever to be able to name in a credible way the presence of the mystery of God within contemporary life, to articulate the historical revelation of God in Christ and to wrestle with the big question about origins and destiny, suffering and death, meaning and apathy, sustainable care of the earth and global warming. Equally, theology needs the community of the Church to ensure that the service of faith and the pastoral needs of people are adequately addressed. A Church without a living and critical theology runs the risk of being surrounded by relativism or fundamentalism. Today in Ireland there is more than a little evidence that both of these extremes are alive and well within Irish Catholicism. At present there is very little room within the Catholic Church for open disagreement and honest debate about the burning issues surrounding ethical questions, the primacy of conscience, the complexity of human relationships in and outside marriage, and the question of God. Theology ought to be taken far more seriously in the life of the institutional Church and also needs to be rehabilitated in the service of the Christian community, the academy and society. Without such rehabilitation we will end up having a Church that is *un-theological* and a theology that is *un-churched*.

A further point about higher education in Ireland is the current largely pro-business, utilitarian and instrumentalist approach to much third-level education. More and more higher education at this time in Ireland is defining itself in terms of serving the economy and supplying graduates for the marketplace. The social, cultural and critical roles of higher education are increasingly sidelined, and if we are to follow the OECD Report on Higher Education (2004) and listen to the voices of some in higher education, then we are heading in the direction of a largely economic, market-driven and utilitarian reduction of the aims of higher education. Of course the service of the information society and the building up of a knowledge economy through research are important and should be to the fore. Equally significant, however, is the promotion of critical thinking, the discussion of a values system in the service of public policy and the common good, and the cultivation of an enquiring mind. These latter do not feature prominently in the current debate about the future of higher education in Ireland. Indeed, there is a disturbing silence about the distinctive contribution that the arts, the humanities and the social sciences can offer to the new Ireland.

There must be a middle way between J.H. Newman and the market, between the legitimate concerns of the OECD report and the equally important values of what was once known as 'a liberal education'. There must be more than just the economic model of higher education in Ireland; other models also exist and must be allowed to exist: liberal, ethical, ecological and interdisciplinary models. Economic, market-driven and commercially competitive criteria must not be allowed to become the sole criteria for the allocation of resources and developments of higher education in Ireland.

There are resources within a Catholic vision of education to engage in this debate, such as the cultivation of the intellectual life as an end in itself, the promotion of the primacy of justice, the development of an ethically and ecologically sensitive social outlook – all of which are hallmarks of a Catholic self-understanding. Equally disturbing within the above emphasis on serving the economy is the relentless emphasis on market-driven success, economic achievement and commercial competition – each of which needs to be balanced by a Christian recognition of the reality of failure as a part of life, the importance of compassion in human relations and the need for solidarity within society.

Further, the Catholic vision of education has a strong sense that there is something truly important about modernity and at the same time something missing within modernity. The Second Vatican Council (1962–1965) embraced modernity in terms of new openness to, dialogue with and a willingness to learn from the modern world, especially in terms of human rights, social justice and religious freedom. However, the Catholic vision of education is uneasy with the dominance of an enlightenment epistemology, with its claim to value free, detached and objective approaches to knowledge as normative. The enlightenment models of rationality and the scientific models of what counts as truth and knowledge can hardly be taken as adequate for appreciating the arts, the humanities and religion. An exclusive emphasis on enlightenment rationalism is usually accompanied by a loss of meaning, the erosion of ethical values and the eclipse of transcendence. Scientific models of truth must be complimented by other paradigms of truth, such as those that recognise the affective, participative and mythological dimensions of human understanding. The enlightenment has bequeathed an understanding of knowledge as that which can be grasped, controlled and manipulated objectively. But there are other models of knowledge in which human beings find themselves drawn, grasped and captivated by otherness and this experience is enhanced not by standing back in a detached manner but by an active, personal engagement in the search for goodness, truth and beauty.

It is the neglect of these other equally valid models of human knowledge in higher education that help us to understand the growing gap between economic progress and social policy, between material advancement and quality of life issues, between success and personal freedom. It would be a great loss to Irish society if the universities ended up becoming only servants of the economy, only instruments of industry and only training centres for the marketplace. It is instructive to note that among the eleven 'objects' of a university in the Universities Act, 1997, the word 'economic' appears only once.[10] What has become of the other 'objects' of the university, such as, for example, the promotion of the social and cultural life of society, the fostering of independent and critical thinking among students and the preservation of the distinctive cultures of Ireland which are mentioned in the Universities Act, 1997? Irish universities and higher education in general are called in this time of national prosperity to enable 'the enlargement of the mind' (J.H. Newman), to expand the ethical capacity of the human and social imagination, and to appreciate the significance of otherness as well as contributing to the growth of the economy.

Increasing levels of funding for research in science and technology in the support of the knowledge-based economy is one of the success stories in higher education in recent times. Irish universities and institutes of technology are now making an important contribution to the advancement of knowledge at both national and international levels and this is something that should be welcomed, encouraged and further supported. And yet in spite of this success, a recent OECD Report suggests that the amount of research going on needs to be increased and the number of Ph.Ds doubled in the years ahead if Ireland is to continue playing a role in advancing knowledge and intellectual property. It would be a loss if these welcome advances in science and technology were not matched by something similar in the arts, the humanities and the social sciences.

Higher education in Ireland is at present in danger of being subverted by the wider culture of unbridled capitalism, the dominance of market-driven ideologies and an instrumentalist approach to knowledge. One of the roles of a university education is surely to critique capitalism, to analyse the underbelly of the market and to resist the reduction of learning and knowledge to an economic commodity. A recent development illustrative of these trends in higher education is the practice of advertising academic posts with the attachment 'the successful candidate will be expected to attract research funding'!

A further feature of higher education is the uncritical acceptance of the project of modernity. The mistake of modernity is the supposition that there is a single, universal, objective rationality to which all must adhere. The *raison d'être* of postmodernity is to object vigorously to the totalising pretensions of modernity. There is much that is wrong with postmodernity – but its objections against the totalising tendency of modernity are instructive: there is no single narrative or discourse. Some will find it difficult to accept this from theolgy because they perceive theology as a totalising subject. However, this common enough perception rests on a misunderstanding of theology. The Christian narrative is historically a self-consciously unfinished narrative. Only those who ignore the eschatological, apophatic (the *via negativa*) and mystical traditions of Christianity will find it difficult to accept that Christianity is an open narrative.

Another aspect of debate about higher education is the confusion surrounding 'the knowledge economy' and 'the knowledge society'. A knowledge economy seeks to link education solely with the service of the economy, whereas a knowledge society has much wider social and cultural aims: analysis of human identity, a critique of social inequalities and the development of the cultural memory and imagination.

In brief, higher education in Ireland needs to become more committed to a multidisciplined and shared search for truth, beauty and goodness, to the promotion of a serious and sustained debate about ethical issues, to the cultivation of intellectual curiosity and imaginative thinking as a value in itself and to the fostering of interrogative modes of learning in all disciplines.

The reason this debate about higher education is so important is that what happens in third-level education quickly influences second-level education. Indeed there are signs already of this utilitarian approach to education creeping into secondary schools with so much emphasis on points for places in college, the demand by the media for achievement-oriented league tables, the mushrooming of competitive grinds schools and the increasing number of second-level students doing part-time work after school hours. It is important that Catholic education resists these developments by offering an alternative and more holistic vision that sees the economy as a means to various ends and not an end in itself.

PART II: ANALYSING SOME OF THE CULTURAL CHANGES WITHIN CONTEMPORARY IRELAND

In part two of my paper I want to outline some of the cultural changes taking place in Ireland that have a bearing on Catholic education today. It is necessary to understand the culture around us before it can be evangelised. As John Paul II remarked several times during his Pontificate: a faith that is not inculturated is not a living faith. So how do we read the cultural changes in modern and postmodern Ireland? Here are some pointers; just pointers!

1   In a very short period of time, Ireland has become a pluralist, multi-cultural and secular society. This means that the Church

must recognise that it no longer has a monopoly on education and can no longer assume to hold a privileged position. From now on Catholic education must recognise itself as one player among many, a voice within a variety of voices, learning to welcome pluralism, value difference and respect otherness. I believe that Catholic education can make a more distinctive contribution to Irish society from within this pluralist, multi-cultural and postmodern context. Catholic education within this new context will become more self-conscious and self-aware of its own particular identity.

2   A second significant shift, indeed a paradigm shift, has taken place within education in the last ten years, and this is best summed up in terms of a move from teaching and training to learning and teaching. Part of this shift includes the momentous move towards information technology as an instrument of learning as well as a recognition of the existence of multiple intelligences among all. Within educational circles, learning is now seen as a lifelong continuum from the cradle to the grave, as evidenced, for example, in the National Framework of Qualifications. Adult education is no longer understood as an optional add-on to schooling but as something intrinsic to the whole of life. This new perception of the centrality of lifelong learning is already affecting the construction of school curricula through the work of the National Framework of Qualifications. This shift, of course, has very significant implications for the way we conceive Catholic education in the future, no longer as something sporadic but ongoing, no longer fixed in the frozen formula of faith but constantly in need of reformulation, no longer terminal with school but self-consciously incomplete and unfinished.

This shift also calls for a change in the philosophy of education operative in Catholic schools. In the future the role of the Catholic school will be to light a fire in the minds of young people so that they will leave second-level education with hungry spirits, restless hearts, inquisitive intellects and creative imaginations. In this way young people going into third-level education will know that there is more to education than just the information society, more to education than just the knowledge-based economy, more to education than just getting a job.

3   Since Ireland has become a wealthy nation through the so-called successes of the Celtic Tiger economy (which incidentally has nothing authentically Celtic about it) a new kind of poverty is now emerging. Those who have everything from a material point of view often end up having nothing from a spiritual point of view. Excessive materialism is itself an expression of a deep spiritual need in the midst of plenty. As a result of this new phenomenon, the search for new spiritualities is alive and well, while institutionalised religion, and in particular institutionalised Christianity, is on the decline. Just go into Waterstones or visit Amazon.com any day and look at the books people are buying. Catholic education in the future will need to bridge the gap that presently exists between spirituality and sacramentality, between the genuine hungers of the secular heart and the liberating Gospel of Jesus Christ, between the restless spirit of so many and the practical wisdom that comes from knowing Christ crucified and risen. We will return to this point in our final section of this paper.

4   There is now a need also to recognise the presence of a new sub-culture that exists outside schools and that often runs counter to what teachers are trying to achieve within the school environment. This sub-culture is best described as one of experimentation in relation to drugs, drink and sexuality. Within this sub-culture young people want to know how far they can go without falling over the edge, how far they can push the body without damaging it, how close they can come to death without dying. This sub-culture outside the school is fuelled by a morbid interest in the world

of the occult, the existence of evil and an extraordinary fascination with violence – all of which are readily available through videos, DVDs and the internet. This subculture is in some instances connected to the breakdown of family life and the absence of a male role model in the home.

5 A further characteristic of contemporary culture in Ireland is the presence of a hidden but deep crisis of faith among a growing number of adults. One expression of this particular crisis can be found in a moving poem entitled 'Missing God' by the relatively young Irish poet, Denis O'Driscoll.[11] The following verses are a sample of the poem:

> Miss Him during the civil wedding
> when, at the blossomy altar
> of the Registrar's desk,
> we wait in vain
> to be fed a line containing words like 'everlasting'
> and 'divine'.
>
> Miss Him when the T.V. Scientist
> explains the cosmos through equations.
>
> Miss Him when a choked voice at
> the crematorium recites the poem
> about fearing no more the heat of the sun.
>
> Miss Him when we stumble on the breast lump
> for the first time and an involuntary prayer
> escapes our lips.
>
> Miss Him when we listen to the prophecy
> of astronomers that the visible galaxies will recede
> as the universe exapands.

Another expression of this crisis is captured rather graphically in an interview given by Seamus Heaney in 2002 where he pointed out:

> I think the dwindling of faith and, secondly, the clerical scandals have bewildered things ... we are still running on an unconscious that is informed by religious values, but I think our youngsters' youngsters won't have that. I think the needles are wobbling.[12]

In my opinion it may be possible to steady the needles before they collapse if we can recover the liberating memory of Jesus Christ and act more imaginatively in the light of that event.

A third expression of this crisis of faith can be found in some of the soul searching and questioning that went on in the media, particularly by Patsy McGarry and Vincent Browne, in relation to God and the 2004 tsunami. What is needed in this new cultural context from Catholic education is the introduction of adults to a genuine experience of God, not as something exceptional, not as the privilege of a few, not as a phenomenon restricted only to 'holy' people, but as that gracious presence that envelops all without exception and sustains the small planet we call 'earth' within the vast cosmos. In this way it might be possible to move beyond an interventionist image of God to a recognition of the Spirit-God as the One in whom we live and move and have our being as pure gift. It is also important in this regard for Catholic education to realise that it does not have all the answers to the burning questions of the day and that, therefore, raising questions, walking in the dark with confidence and struggling with faith are also a significant part of the Catholic experience.

CONCRETE PROPOSALS FOR THE FUTURE

In the light of this review of what I see going on in education and in the light of the above broad description of cultural changes in modern Ireland, I now want to outline some of the challenges facing Catholic education in the future. In particular, I want to suggest by way of conclusion in summary fashion some concrete proposals for Catholic education.

1 By far the most important and most urgent proposal is the need to introduce parish-based, ongoing programmes of evangelisation in and through a process of adult faith formation and/or adult religious education. The specific orientation of these programmes of New Evangelisation ought to be a matter for determination at local level to reflect local needs. What Catholic education needs to do most of all in Ireland at this time is to introduce people to a process of lifelong Christian learning and lifelong faith development. What has happened in the last thirty years concerning school catechesis and religious education now needs to happen in the area of adult Christian education in terms of resources, personnel and provision. This does not mean that the Church abandons present involvement with schools and the support of principals, religious educators and chaplains. Instead it demands that the Church now looks in both directions, by continuing to support schools while at the same time addressing the ongoing educational and spiritual needs of adult Catholics in parishes. If this can be done, and I believe it can be done by recovering the memory of Jesus and exercising the religious imagination, then the good work going on in primary and secondary schools will bear real fruit in the future and adult communities of faith will be more vibrant and active. A good start in new, parish-based programmes of religious education signalling what can be done has been made through the programme *Do this in Memory* by Maeve Mahon and Fr Martin Delaney in the dioceses of Kildare and Leighlin and Ossory,[13] and further examples of good practice are also available in other dioceses.

133

This huge challenge of lifelong learning facing Catholic education in Ireland should be approached not in *ad hoc* manner but in a strategically planned way; not in terms of offering a few lectures here and there but according to the principles and methods specific to adult education; not by someone who knows a little theology but by professionally qualified personnel in the theory and practice of adult education.

2   A second concrete proposal relates to the need to act decisively in relation to the provision of a professional chaplaincy service in voluntary secondary schools. I think I have already said enough about this matter and sufficient work has been done to advance it immediately.

3   A third proposal concerns the importance of promoting continuing professional development of Catholic teachers, especially those in the following categories:

- Principals and deputy principals in leadership positions;
- Catechists and religious educators;
- Chaplains and coordinators of chaplaincy services.

At present there is insufficient educational support or spiritual nourishment of those in Catholic schools who are expected to lead in culturally difficult times and carry the burden in the heat of the day. In bygone days there were religious communities in the background supporting the leaders in Catholic schools.

4   A fourth challenge for Catholic education is to enter into a new relationship of cooperation and partnership with the State and its agencies of education. This will require a movement from a hermeneutics of suspicion to a hermeneutics of collaboration and goodwill on both sides. In this context it will be necessary for the Church to speak with one voice representing both prophetic and institutional wings of Catholic identity, bringing together the Catholic

bishops and CORI into a new strategic alliance and relationship, already begun at this conference!

5   A fifth proposal is the need to correct and transform existing caricatures and stereotypes of Catholic education operative at present in the public domain. It needs to be said that Catholic education is not about control but about offering a vision of life inspired by Jesus of Nazareth; is not about indoctrination but about opening windows of wonder and igniting a search for wisdom; is not something exclusive to Catholics but inclusive and welcoming towards all to 'come and see'; is not sectarian but radically ecumenical and formally committed to inter-religious dialogue. Concerning this last point, it should be acknowledged clearly that ecumenism is not an optional extra within Catholic education; it is rather a part of the teaching of the Catholic Church since the Second Vatican Council. Likewise, respect for and engagement with the elements of 'grace and truth' and the action of the Holy Spirit that exist in other religions, especially the monotheistic religions of Judaism and Islam, is also an intrinsic part of Catholic education.[14] This dialogue with other religions is not about dumbing down differences but is rather a process of discovering one's own Catholic identity through encounter with the other, seeking points of mutual convergences wherever they exist and acknowledging with honesty the presence of theological differences. To be religious in the future will of necessity require that we be inter-religious. It may well come as a surprise to some to learn that the Catholic Church has been to the fore in promoting inter-religious exchanges since the Second Vatican Council. Nobody has been more innovative and prophetic in this regard than the late John Paul II, bringing together the major religions of the world at Assisi in 1986 and again in 2002. Consider also his prophetic actions throughout the Jubilee Year: for example his visit to the Wailing Wall in Jerusalem and other prophetic gestures vis-á-vis Islam. In my

opinion his teaching and actions in the area of inter-religious dialogue are a central plank of his legacy and they have enormous implications for Catholic education, and Catholics, therefore, should be leading the way in this regard in the newly emerging multi-cultural Ireland.

6 A sixth proposal arising out of our analysis of cultural changes relates to the new interest in spirituality. There is such a thing as a distinctive Catholic spirituality, which we can only hint at here. Catholic education needs to introduce adults to the rich tradition of mysticism that is a part of the heritage of Christian spirituality. Catholic education should remember what Karl Rahner once said: the Christian of tomorrow will be nothing if he or she is not a mystic. When Rahner speaks of mystical experience, he does not mean some exceptional, unusual or rare religious experience; instead what Rahner has in mind is an experience of God available to all. At the same time, however, we must advance Rahner's advice by highlighting that the Christian of tomorrow must also be able to link this mystical experience with the political. A fundamental unity exists within the bible and much of the Christian tradition on the close relationship that obtains between the mystical and the political, between the personal experience of God and prophetic action for justice within society, between personal spirituality and public witness. The Judeo-Christian tradition of spirituality refuses to allow faith to be sidelined by secular authority or privatised by particular political interests. It is in the interest of 'the powers and principalities' of this world to sideline and silence Christian faith and spirituality. At this strange time of history in Ireland, Christians through their spirituality are called to be prophetic nuisances in the public square. An additional aspect of Catholic spirituality is the link with sacraments, especially the Eucharist. A eucharistic spirituality lifts us out of our isolation into a communion

with others 'in Christ' and carries with it a commitment to service symbolised by the washing of the feet.

7 One final proposal. The Catholic voice in Ireland is now one voice within a pluralism of educational voices. To engage with this reality of pluralism one must have a sense of one's own identity. Catholic education, therefore, is not about being all things to all women and men to such an extent that one ends up standing for nothing. Instead it must be recognised that it is only possible to engage fruitfully with pluralism from within a specific tradition. Dialogue within a pluralist situation is not about melting down differences to a bland blob; instead it means that everyone brings something of value to the table and comes away enriched through the encounter with difference. At the Second Vatican Council, the Church claimed to offer something of value to individuals and society – but it also acknowledged explicitly that it learned from the world and benefited from the antagonisms of those who disagreed with it.[15]

By way of conclusion I want to return to my opening remarks. There we saw that Catholic education must seek to unite memory and imagination. In particular, Catholic education is committed to keeping alive the liberating, healing and subversive memory of Jesus as the Christ, especially in relation to the wisdom teaching, table fellowship and proclamation of the reign of God by Jesus. On the other hand, that historical memory of Jesus now active through the Spirit in the Church and the world must become inserted imaginatively into our understanding of the world today. The memory of Jesus will have a paschal, sacramental and eschatological influence on the shape of the human imagination in the twenty-first century.

Notes

1 Quotation taken from *European Ethics Network Vademecum 2002-2003: Socrates/Erasmus Thematic Network,* J. Verstraeten and Maria Duffy (eds), Leuven, 2002, p. 2

2 Mary Warnock, *Imagination,* London: Faber and Faber, 1976, pp. 9–10.

3 'Why Sorrow', *Patrick Kavanagh: The Complete Poems,* Newbridge, 1972/1984, p. 176.

4 *Pastoral Constitution on the Church in the Modern World,* n. 4.

5 See *Teaching Religion in the Primary School: Issues and Challenges* (INTO, 2003).

6 'The Ethos of the Catholic School', *Teaching Religion in the Primary School* (INTO, 2003), p. 111.

7 See report by Dr Muiris Houston in *The Irish Times,* 15 February 2006, p. 2.

8 Marie Cassidy, *The Irish Times,* 15 February 2006, p. 5.

9 See *The Irish Times,* 10 August 2006, p. 8.

10 *Universities Act, 1997*: 11.

11 Dennis O'Driscoll, 'Missing God', *Exemplary Damages,* London: Anvil Poetry Press, 2002, pp. 29–31.

12 An interview in the *Irish Independent Weekend,* 16 November 2002, p. 9.

13 Veritas, 2004.

14 See the documents *Nostra aetate* and *Ad gentes* of the Second Vatican Council (1965) and commentary by Dermot A. Lane, '*Nostra aetate*: Encountering other Religious, Enriching the Theological Imagination' in *Vatican II: Facing the 21st Century: Historical and Theological Perspectives,* Dermot Lane and Brendan Leahy (eds), Dublin: Veritas, 2006, pp. 202–36.

15 See *GS,* n. 41–4.

The Religious Dimension of Education in Irish Second-Level Schools at the Start of the Third Millennium

Andrew G. McGrady

INTRODUCTION

Second-level schooling in Ireland is undergoing a period of transition in response to theological, educational, cultural, demographic, legal and constitutional change. This finds expression in increasing pluralism, new management structures for Catholic schools, changing patterns of religiosity among pupils and parents, changing patterns of religious commitment among school staff and increased parental choice in school selection. In Ireland, secondary schools mainly consist of three sectors: voluntary secondary schools (largely Catholic schools under the trusteeship of religious congregations), vocational schools and community colleges (managed by Vocational Education Committees at county level) and community and comprehensive schools (managed on behalf of the State by Boards of Management which include religious orders and / or bishops). In recent decades the decline in the number of members of religious orders, an increase in the number of lay teaching staff, a movement towards the appointment of lay men and women to the position of school principal and the amalgamation of schools, for instance by the merging of existing single-sex voluntary Catholic secondary schools with vocational schools to form co-educational community schools, has brought the question of the distinctive character of the Catholic school in Ireland into greater prominence.

This paper presents a summary of the Catholic Church's theological and philosophical vision for the religious dimension of education in both Catholic schools and indeed for the full human development of pupils in all schools. The paper draws upon documentation emanating from the Magisterium and from the Catholic Church in Ireland. It does not offer a critical appraisal of the state of Catholic schools in Ireland, but, in the context of seeking to articulate a vision and mission for Catholic schools, raises issues related to school identity, school leadership, partnership between the school, parents and the wider Catholic faith community, the nature and purpose of religious education and its link with faith formation, the integrated curriculum, the role of teachers in Catholic schools ecumenical and inter-religious dialogue and, most importantly, the impact of all of these factors on the full human development of each pupil.

Since the Second Vatican Council the nature and purpose of the Catholic school, and its place within wider Catholic education, has been the subject of continuing and substantive reflection. There have been a series of documents from the Magisterium which have either informed the approach to the Catholic school or which have explicitly addressed it. In October 1965 the second Vatican Council promulgated the Declaration on Christian Education, *Gravissimum educationis*, a document which must be situated in the context of the ecclesiology of other conciliar documents, most notably the Dogmatic Constitution on the Church (1965, *Lumen gentium*), the Pastoral Constitution on the Church in the Modern World (1965, *Gaudium et spes*), the Dogmatic Constitution on Divine Revelation (*Dei Verbum*), the Decree on the Apostolate of the Laity (1965, *Apostolicam actuositatem*), the Decree on Missionary Activity (*Ad gentes divinitus*), the Declaration on Non-Christian Religions (*Nostra aetate*), the Decree on Ecumenism (1965,

Unitatis redintegratio) and the Declaration on Religious Liberty (1965, *Dignitatis humanae*). The Apostolic Exhortation of Pope Paul VI *Evangelii nuntiandi* (1975) and those of Pope John Paul II, *Catechesi tradendae* (1979), *Fides et ratio* (1998) and *Novo Millennio ineunte* (2001), are also of particular importance.

To these must be added documents promulgated by various Vatican congregations. The Congregation for Clergy (which also oversees the work of catechists and teachers of religion) promulgated the first edition of the *General Catechetical Directory* (*Directorium catechisticum general*) in 1971 and a revised edition, the *General Directory for Catechesis*, in 1997. The Congregation for Catholic Education promulgated a series of documents addressing specific aspects of Catholic education. These are: *The Catholic School* (1977), *Lay Catholics in Schools: Witnesses to the Faith* (1982), *Educational Guidance in Human Love: Outlines for Sex Education* (1983), *The Religious Dimension of Education in the Catholic School* (1988), *The Catholic School on the Threshold of the Third Millennium* (1997) and *Consecrated Persons and their Mission in Schools* (2002). *The Code of Canon Law* (1985) and *Catechism of the Catholic Church* (1994) are also important documents of relevance to Catholic education.

There have also been a number of documents published by the Irish Catholic Bishops' Conference and its constituent commissions. The most important of these are: *Handing on the Faith in the Home* (1979), the *Syllabus for the Religious Education of Catholic Pupils in Post-Primary Schools* (1982), the *Submission to the New Ireland Forum* (1984) and the *Guidelines for the Faith Formation and Development of Catholic Students* (1999).[1] Other important documents are the *Management Board Members' Handbook* (Catholic Primary School Managers' Association, revised 2000) and the *Irish Catholic Bishops' Report on the Situation of Catechesis in Ireland* for the *Congregatio Pro Doctrina Fidei et Congegatio Pro Clericis* in Rome (December 2001). Other documents of importance in the Irish context are the Constitution and the 1998 Education Act.

AGENCIES OF RELIGIOUS FORMATION

The Church situates her reflections on schooling within the broader context of her educational mission which involves a wider group of agencies, most importantly the local parish and the family. 'Catholic education begins and is nurtured in the home, it is taught and fostered by the schools, and it lives and matures through the parish'.[2] Thus, the school is only one agency, though a vital agency, of education and must work in collaboration with the other agencies. The Irish Catholic Bishops' Conference is aware of the need for initiatives in this area:

> Partnership and shared responsibility are the kernel of a renewed catechetical vision of the home, school and parish community working together in support of the young person's journey towards maturity of faith ... The school community cannot and should not be expected to carry the responsibility for faith formation and development entirely on its own. Without such partnership, catechesis, in its fullest sense, is not possible.[3]

In their 2002 report to Rome 'The Situation of Catechesis in Ireland', the Bishops stated (p. 7):

> It will be seen that of the three levels of religious education in Ireland, school-based learning is by far the strongest. They are in the formal schooling areas of primary and post-primary education. The Church in Ireland can be proud of this historical involvement in Irish education. However, in the area of adult religious education fewer enterprises have needed greater attention.

They further quoted Kennedy 2000 that 'the classroom is a place of positive religious discourse and experience' while 'the home is a space where there is little or no religious discourse and experience' and 'the parish is a space of diminishing religious discourse and experience'.[4] This is not a new concern; Lane (1991) noted that in Ireland 'schools have become so important in the education of young people that other equally important agents of Catholic education, such as the family and the parish [have] tended to let the school carry the overall responsibility'.[5] Our reflections on Catholic schools therefore need to be situated in this wider context of partnership between the family, the parish and the school as agencies of religious formation.

THE THEOLOGICAL BASIS OF CATHOLIC EDUCATION

In her most recent document, *Consecrated Persons and their Mission in Schools* (2002), the Church stated that to educate is to evangelise (CPMS 6). In all her reflections on education and schooling the Church states that her duty to educate arises from her responsibility of 'announcing the way of salvation to all men, of communicating the life of Christ to those who believe, and, in her unfailing solicitude, of assisting men to be able to come to the fullness of this life' (GE 3). In the subsequent document on evangelisation, *Evangelii nuntiandi* (paragraph 18), Paul VI stated 'to evangelise is to bring the Good News to all aspects of humanity and, through its influence, to transform it from within, making humanity itself into something new'. This is subsequently repeated; for instance RDECS 66 states, 'the mission of the Church is to evangelise, for the interior transformation and the renewal of humanity'. Such promotion of full human development is seen in Christocentric terms:

> the Church is bound as a mother to give to these children of hers an education by which their whole life can be imbued with the spirit of Christ and at the same time do all she can to promote for all peoples the complete perfection of the human person, the good of earthly

society and the building of a world that is more human. (GE3)

The Catholic School (1977) dwells further on evangelisation. Catholic education is to 'serve humanity until it reaches its fullness in Christ' (CS 6). This imposes on the Church the duty to evangelise in particular those who have been baptised before a full catechesis has been provided. The Church 'must proclaim the good news of salvation to all, generate new creatures in Christ through Baptism, and train them to live knowingly as children of God' (CS 7). The Catholic school tries to create 'a climate[6] in which the pupils' faith will gradually mature and enable [the pupil] to assume the responsibility placed on him by Baptism' (CS 47). The role of evangelisation is the full development of the human person, 'the incarnation of the Christian message in the lives of men and women' (LCS 31). A prime means for this are Catholic schools that the Church establishes 'because she considers them as a privileged means of promoting the formation of the whole man, since the school is a centre in which a specific concept of the world, of man and of history is developed and conveyed' (CS 8).

Thus, the key theological principles initially evident in GE and subsequently developed in later documents are:

1 The Church's involvement in education arises from its 'salvific mission' (in subsequent documentation this is more formally linked with evangelisation);

2 Catholic schools therefore have an ecclesial identity being manifestations of the Church itself;

3 Evangelisation requires an engagement not just with individuals but with culture itself;

4 Authentic education relates to full human development;

5 Which is nurtured by immersion in a community;

6 And ultimately full human development can only be understood in Christocentric terms.

144

THE CONSTITUTIONAL AND LEGAL POSITION OF CATHOLIC SCHOOLS IN THE REPUBLIC OF IRELAND

While the legal and constitutional position of Catholic schools is not the main focus of this paper, it nevertheless constitutes the socio-cultural context in which Catholic schools operate and accordingly a brief overview will be provided here. The constitutional and legal position in Ireland is highly hospitable to Catholic schools; in fact, all faith schools, including Catholic schools, operate in what is probably the most favourable climate within Europe.

Ireland does not have a secular constitution. Article 6 of the Irish Constitution respects religion and acknowledges God as the source of its authority. Article 44 of the Constitution (concerning religion) states:

1 The State acknowledges that the homage of public worship is due to Almighty God. It shall hold his name in reverence, and shall respect and honour religion.

2 Freedom of conscience and the free profession and practice of religion are, subject to public order and morality, guaranteed to every citizen.

3 The State guarantees not to endow any religion.

4 The State shall not impose any disabilities or make any discrimination on the ground of religious profession, belief or status.

5 Legislation providing State aid for schools shall not discriminate between schools under the management of different religious denominations, nor be such as to affect prejudicially the right of any child to attend a school receiving public money without attending religious instruction at that school.

6 Every religious denomination shall have the right to manage its own affairs, own, acquire and administer property,

movable and immovable, and maintain institutions for religious or charitable purposes.

7 The property of any religious denomination or any educational institution shall not be diverted save for necessary works of public utility and on payment of compensation.

The relationship between the State and the Church in the area of education is further enshrined in Article 42 of the Constitution (concerning education) which states that:

1 The State acknowledges that the primary and natural educator of the child is the family and guarantees to respect the inalienable right and duty of parents to provide, according to their means, for the religious and moral, intellectual, physical and social education of their children.

2 Parents shall be free to provide this education in their homes or in private schools or in schools recognised or established by the State.

3 The State shall not oblige parents in violation of their conscience and lawful preference to send their children to schools established by the State, or to any particular type of school designated by the State.

4 The State shall, however, as guardian of the common good, require in view of actual conditions that the children receive a certain minimum education, moral, intellectual and social.

5 The State shall provide for free primary education and shall endeavour to supplement and give reasonable aid to private and corporate educational initiative and, when the public good requires it, provide other educational facilities or institutions with due regard, however, for the rights of parents, especially in the matter of religious and moral formation.

6 In exceptional cases, where the parents for physical or moral reasons fail in their duty towards their children, the State as

guardian of the common good, by appropriate means, shall endeavour to supply the place of the parents, but always with due regard for the natural and imprescriptible rights of the child.

We can briefly summarise the constitutional position as follows. The primary responsibility to educate rests with parents rather than the State. Parents may come together with others to provide for the education of their children. The State has the responsibility to provide for such education. The Church's right to establish schools is acknowledged by the Constitution as is the right of parents to withdraw their child from the religious instruction provided by the school.

The Education Act (1998) explicitly addresses the issue of the distinctive ethos of the schools and states that a Board of Management shall:

> uphold, and be accountable to the patron for so upholding, the characteristic spirit of the school as determined by the cultural, educational, moral, religious, social, linguistic and spiritual values and traditions which inform and are characteristic of the objectives and conduct of the school, and at all times act in accordance with any Act of the Oireachtas or instrument relating to the establishment or operation of the school *and* 'consult with and keep the patron informed of decisions and proposals of the board'. Section 15 (2) (b) & (c)

In the Irish context churches and religious communities have the right to appoint and remove teaching staff; this applies not only to teachers of RE but also to all teachers in a Catholic voluntary secondary school. In the Supreme Court judgment in Re Art. 26 and the Employment Equality Bill 1996, the court held that section 37(1) was constitutional. This Bill (and the subsequent Act) prohibits discrimination against a person on many grounds including religious. Section 37 (1) of the Employment Equality Bill 1996 reads:

> A religious, educational or medical institution which is under the direction or control of a body established for religious purposes or whose objectives include the provision of services in an environment which promotes certain religious values shall not be taken to discriminate against a person ... if
>
> a it gives more favourable treatment, on the religion ground, to an employee or a prospective employee over that person where it is reasonable to do so in order to maintain the religious ethos of the institution, or
>
> b it takes action which is reasonably necessary to prevent an employee or a prospective employee from undermining the religious ethos of the institution.

Concerning the nature of religious education, a recent judgment of the Supreme Court is of particular interest. In 1996, using the constitutional prohibition against the endowment of religion as its basis, the 'Campaign to Separate Church and State Incorporated' took a case against the Irish government and the four Catholic archbishops to prevent the extension of the existing State payment of chaplains in vocational schools to community schools. The Supreme Court rejected the claim on following basis:

> While the effect of Art 44.2 is to outlaw the 'establishment' by the State of any religion, State aid to a denominational school for educational purposes is not an 'endowment' within the meaning of Art 44.2.2. Parental rights to provide for the religious and moral education of their children involve the right to have religious education, beyond mere religious instruction, in the

schools their children attend. The role of a chaplain is to help provide this extra dimension to the religious education of children. Therefore, payment by the State of chaplains in community schools is a manifestation, under modern conditions, of principles approved by Articles 44 and 42 of the Constitution.[7]

The ruling is of interest not only because of the extension of the approval of the payment of chaplains but because it refers to a parental right for the provision of religious education, defines religious education as going beyond 'mere religious instruction' and relates the role of the chaplain to the 'extra-dimension' of religious education thereby acknowledging that religious education extends beyond the classroom-centered religious education lesson.

In the Irish context an influential definition of the Catholic school is that provided in the Management Board Members' Handbook[8] for primary schools which states that:

A Roman Catholic School (which is established in connection with the Minister) aims at promoting the full and harmonious development of all aspects of the person of the pupil: intellectual, physical, cultural, moral and spiritual, including a living relationship with God and with other people. The school models and promotes a philosophy of life inspired by belief in God and in the life, death and resurrection of Jesus Christ. The Catholic school provides religious education for the pupils in accordance with the doctrines, practices and tradition of the Roman Catholic Church and promotes the formation of the pupils in the Catholic Faith.

THE IDENTITY OF THE CATHOLIC SCHOOL

The question 'What is the ethos or distinctive characteristic spirit of the Catholic school?' is increasingly important throughout the western world in general and for second-level schools in Ireland in particular. Based upon socio-cultural dialogue and upon its theology of education, GE 8 describes the distinctive spirit, or ethos, of the Catholic school:

> No less than other schools does the Catholic school pursue cultural goals and the human formation of youth. But its proper function is to create for the school community a special atmosphere animated by the Gospel spirit of freedom and charity, to help youth grow according to the new creatures they were made through baptism as they develop their own personalities, and finally to order the whole of human culture to the news of salvation so that the knowledge the students gradually acquire of the world, life and man is illumined by faith. So indeed the Catholic school, while it is open, as it must be, to the situation of the contemporary world, leads its students to promote efficaciously the good of the earthly city and also prepares them for service in the spread of the Kingdom of God, so that by leading an exemplary apostolic life they become, as it were, a saving leaven in the human community. (GE 8)

In its introduction, *The Catholic School* (CS 1) contextualises reflections on education within the serious problems which are an integral part of Christian education in a pluralistic society (CS 2). The aim of the document is explicitly stated as being to consider 'the nature and distinctive characteristics' of the Catholic school (CS 2). 'The real problem facing the Catholic school is to identify and lay down the conditions necessary for it to fulfil its mission' (CS 64). This is particularly urgent since 'often what is perhaps fundamentally lacking among Catholics who work in a school is a clear realisation of the identity of a Catholic school and the courage to follow all the consequences of its uniqueness' (CS 66).

In its introduction (par. 1), *The Religious Dimension of Education in the Catholic School* again quotes GE 8 regarding it as the foundation to a contemporary understanding of Catholic education and comments that 'what makes the Catholic School distinctive is its religious dimension'. It continues to identify four aspects constituting such a religious dimension: the educational climate, the personal development of each student, the relationship established between culture and the Gospel, and the illumination of all knowledge in the light of faith. RDECS defines school climate as 'the sum total of the different components at work in the school which interact with one another in such a way as to create favourable conditions for a formation process' (RDECS 24).

CSTTM also returns to the issue of the distinctive character of the Catholic school. CSTTM 3 calls for 'courageous renewal on the part of the Catholic school', a renewal that includes the duty for the school to be an agent of evangelisation. In an apt comment it notes, 'the Catholic school must be able to speak for itself effectively and convincingly'. CSTTM 4 also focuses attention on 'the nature and distinctive characteristics of a school which would present itself as Catholic', and identifies the six fundamental characteristics of the Catholic school as:

1 Being a place of integral education of the human person through a clear educational project of which Christ is the foundation;
2 Having an ecclesial identity;
3 Having a cultural identity;
4 Basing its educational mission on the work of love;
5 Being of service to society;
6 Being an educating community characterised by distinctive traits.

Each of these six attributes interacts with each other; they should not be regarded as discrete or separate. Together they provide a useful schema for summarising the Church's approach to the Catholic school.

Characteristic 1: A Place of Integral Education of the Human Person Founded on Christ

Catholic education is based upon a distinctive incarnational anthropology that sees Christ as the paradigm of the human person. The incarnate Christ not only reveals the fullness of Divinity, he also reveals the fullness of redeemed humanity. CSTTM 9 states 'the Catholic school sets out to be a school for the human person and of human persons'. It quotes John Paul II's 1991 statement that '... the promotion of the human person is the goal of the Catholic school'[9] and affirms that 'all human values find their fulfillment and unity in Christ'.[10] The document returns to this theme in its concluding remarks (CSTTM 21) when it again quotes John Paul II's statement that 'man is the primary and fundamental way for the Church, the way traced out by Christ himself'.[11] The doctrine of the incarnation is thus the starting point for any understanding of Catholic schooling, as it is for a true Christian humanism.

The human person as free, rational and relational. The view of the learner that we hold directly affects every aspect of education. 'Each type of education is influenced by a particular concept of what it means to be a human person' (LCS 18). CSTTM 10 reaffirms that 'education always presupposes and involves a definite concept of man and life'. A profound respect for the dignity of the human person that underpins a Catholic philosophy of education is particularly evident in the Church's documentation. 'A human being has a dignity and a greatness exceeding that of all other creatures: a work of God that has been elevated to the supernatural order as a child of God, and therefore having both a divine origin and an eternal destiny which transcend this physical universe.'[12] 'It is what a person is rather than what a person has that counts' (GS 35).

Catholic tradition cherishes the freedom of the human person who is being evangelised through education. It rejects the stimulus–response view evident in conditioning models of learning and instead offers an invitation–response relationship based upon grace. 'Human beings are fundamentally free; they are not the property of the state or of any human organisation'. GS 9 proclaimed 'the act of faith is of its very nature a free act'. Christian faith is offered 'in the nature of a gift: though offered insistently and urgently, it cannot be imposed' (LCS 28). Education can thus be seen as 'the acquisition, growth and possession of freedom' (CPMS 52). The school invites each student to 'free him/herself from the conditionings that prevent him/her from fully living as a person, to form him/herself into a strong and responsible personality, capable of making free and consistent choices' (CPMS 52). To view the human as free is to adopt an intrinsically religious view of the human person. Increasingly in western schools 'the religious dimension of a person has become a *lost link*, not only in the typically educational sphere of schools, but also in the more extensive formative process that began in the family' (CPMS 52).

Within Catholic tradition the human person is defined by his *rationality*, that is by 'his intelligent and free nature', and by his *relational nature*, that is by 'his relationship with other persons' (CPMS 35). Human persons develop through authentic relationships; 'living with others involves both the level of the being of the human person – man/woman – and the ethical level of his acting' (CPMS 35). At the heart of such relationships is openness to the other, an ongoing invitation to personal transcendence; 'the existence of a person appears therefore as a call to the duty to exist for one another' (CPMS 35). Thus, 'the human person experiences his humanity to the extent that he is able to participate in the humanity of the other' (CPMS 36).

The view of the human person is of course intimately linked with the understanding of the Church of the purpose of life, 'Either implicit or explicit reference to a determined attitude to life ... is unavoidable in education because it comes into every decision that is made' (CS 29). The entire process of education, therefore, is a service to the individual students, helping each one to achieve the most complete formation possible' (RDECS 63). During adolescence the school must help pupils to gradually acquire a mature understanding of all that is implied in the concept of *person*: 'intelligence and will, freedom and feelings, the capacity to be an active and creative agent, a being endowed with both rights and duties, capable of interpersonal relationships, called to a specific mission in the world' (RDECS 55).

Such a profound emphasis on the individual human person, called to relationship with the other, has important implications for the manner in which educators conceptualise the relationship between the individual and wider culture and society. The humanism upon which Catholic education is based 'advocates a vision of society centred on the human person and his inalienable rights, on the values of justice and peace, on a correct relationship between individuals, society and the State, on the logic of solidarity and subsidiarity. It is a humanism capable of giving a soul to economic progress itself, so that it may be directed to the *promotion of each individual and of the whole person*' (CPMS 60).[13]

Education as 'unfolding' and 'becoming'. CSTTM 10 notes that an integral view of education is obscured by the 'tendency to reduce education to its purely technical and practical aspects' and by conceptualising education in terms of didactic skills rather than by reflecting on 'the essence of education'. The Church has repeatedly rejected a pragmatic, instrumental or reductionist approach to education which focuses on the provision of life-skills, particularly those of relevance to market capitalism. The aim of education (not just Catholic education) is the full formation of the human person 'in the pursuit of his ultimate end and of the good of the societies of which, as man, he is a member, and in whose obligations, as an adult, he will share' (GE 1). Education is a process of formation that is wider than skills acquisition; such formation involves 'becoming' and 'unfolding'. Thus, education is not primarily the imposition of something from without but 'the development of man from within, freeing him from that conditioning which would prevent him from becoming a "fully integrated human being"' (CS 29). 'We need to think of Christian education as a movement or a growth process directed towards an ideal goal which goes beyond the limitations of anything human' (RDECS 98). Thus, the school must always be concerned with 'the growth of the whole person' (CS 29). While the school must develop 'with special care the intellectual faculties' it must also form the 'ability to judge rightly, to hand on the cultural legacy of previous generations, to foster a sense of values, to prepare for professional life' (GE 5). Teachers have a privileged role to play in such unfolding; the core of that role is that of a 'personalised accompanying' of the individual pupil (CPMS 62).

The spiritual, the religious and the ethical are therefore essential components of the educational enterprise (CS 30). The school seeks to develop 'persons who are responsible and inner-directed, capable of choosing freely in conformity with their conscience ... The school is an institution where young people gradually learn to open themselves up to life as it is, and to create in themselves a definite attitude to life as it should be' (CS 31). Education should seek to free pupils from everything that diminishes them as human beings, developing them from within (CS 29). In developing the physical, moral and intellectual endowments of the pupil, education promotes 'a mature sense of responsibility', 'true freedom' and equips the learner with the social skills necessary to promote the 'common good'.

Education has an essential religious dimension. A fragmented view of education is often expressed in the claim that schools must be 'neutral' with respect to religious belief. The Church in its documentation rejects such a view: a complete education necessarily includes a religious dimension. 'Religion is an effective contribution to the development of other aspects of a personality in the measure in which it is integrated into general education' (CS 19). Schools, therefore, cannot be neutral with respect to religion since religion 'focuses on the human person in his or her integral, transcendent, historical identity'.

A christocentric anthropology. Of course what makes a Catholic anthropology of education particularly distinctive is its incarnational and Christocentric focus: 'it is only in the mystery of the Word made flesh that the mystery of man truly becomes clear' (GS 6). This key theological principle was evident in *Gravissimum educationis*; the Council proclaimed that Christ is 'the goal of human history, focal point of the longings of history and of civilization, centre of the human race, joy of every heart and the answer to all its yearnings' (GS 45). It is in him that we can see 'the truth about the human person' (CPMS 1). The 1977 document on *The Catholic School* reiterated that 'the Catholic school is committed to the development of the whole man, since in Christ, the Perfect Man, all human values find their fulfilment and unity ... He is the one who ennobles humanity, gives meaning to human life, and is the Model which the Catholic school offers to its pupils' (CS 35). Like every school, the Catholic school has as its aim the critical communication of human culture and the total formation of the individual (CS 36). Thus, the view of full human development that inspires the Catholic school is derived from 'a Christian concept of life centred on Jesus Christ' (CS 33). This is the central focus since 'Christ is the foundation of the whole educational enterprise in a Catholic school' (CS 34). 'The Catholic school loses its purpose without constant reference to the Gospel and a frequent encounter with Christ. It derives all the energy necessary for its educational work from him and thus 'creates in the school community an atmosphere permeated with the Gospel spirit of freedom and love'.[14] In this setting the pupil experiences his dignity as a person before he knows its definition (CS 55). The purpose of education is not to promote power but 'a fuller understanding of, and communion with man, events and things. Knowledge is not to be considered as a means of material prosperity and success, but as a call to serve and to be responsible for others' (CS 56).

Paragraphs 74–81 of the RDECS present an outline for an organic presentation of the Christian event and the Christian message. Although this outline has been superseded by the publication of the *Catechism of the Catholic Church* this section provides further insight into a Christocentric anthropology. RDECS 76 notes that as pupils explore the mystery of Christ they 'discover the true value of the human person: loved by God, with a mission on earth and a destiny that is immortal. As a result, they learn the virtues of self-respect and self-love, and of love for others – a love that is universal'. RDECS 82 states that 'each truth of faith has educational and ethical implications', while RDECS 84 continues:

> the human person is present in all the truths of faith: created in 'the image and likeness' of God; elevated by God to the dignity of a child of God; unfaithful to God in original sin, but redeemed by Christ; a temple of the Holy Spirit; a member of the Church; destined to eternal life.

A good summary of the Christocentric approach to Catholic education is that provided by the Irish Catholic bishops: 'the content of catechesis should be Christ-centred while the method of teaching should be student-centred.'[15]

Characteristic 2: The Ecclesial Identity of the Catholic School

The second defining characteristic of the Catholic school is its ecclesial identity; it is 'at the heart of the Church' (CSTTM 11). The ecclesial identity of the school was developed in the

157

document *The Religious Dimension of Education in the Catholic School*, which saw the school as a pastoral instrument of the Church: 'its specific pastoral service consists in mediating between faith and culture' (RDECS 31). The Catholic school is a 'genuine and proper instrument of the Church. It is a place of evangelisation' (RDECS 33). This involves a reciprocal commitment of the school to the Church and the Church to the school: 'just as the Church is present in the school, so the school is present in the Church' (RDECS 44). CSTTM 12 notes that the Catholic school should provide a 'genuine experience of Church'.

A community based on freedom and love. An immediate implication of the ecclesial status of the school is that it must create and sustain a community. The Council highlighted the paradigm of the Church as a community of the people of God, rather than an institution. The ecclesiology of the Council was based upon the notion of *communio*. This notion is carried forward to an understanding of the Catholic School. RDECS 31, referring to GE 6, states that the important advance of the Council was 'the transition from the school as an institution to the school as a community'. The 'Catholic school ... must be a community' since 'Christian faith, in fact, is born and grows inside a community' (CS 53). 'The community aspect of the Catholic school is necessary because of the nature of the faith and not simply because of the nature of man and the nature of the educational process which is common to every school' (CS 54). The concept of the school as an 'educational community ... is one of the most enriching developments for the contemporary school' (LCS 22). In *The Religious Dimension of Education in the Catholic School*, there is an insistent emphasis that the school is a community 'permeated by the Gospel spirit of freedom and love' (RDECS 25, 26, 38–39). Such an understanding places a huge responsibility upon the school because to the school community the students' 'youth has been entrusted' (RDECS

26). By being an educational community the school 'is itself a school. It teaches one how to be a member of the wider social communities and ... what it means to be a member of that great community which is the Church' (LCS 22).

The Catholic School notes that by establishing and sustaining such a community the Church undertakes a real service both to the individual and to wider society:

> Today especially one sees a world which clamours for solidarity and yet experiences the rise of new forms of individualism. Society can take note from the Catholic school that it is possible to create true communities out of a common effort for the common good. In the pluralistic society of today the Catholic school, moreover, by maintaining an institutional Christian presence in the academic world, proclaims by its very existence the enriching power of the faith as the answer to the enormous problems that afflict mankind. Above all, it is called to render a humble loving service to the Church by ensuring that she is present in the scholastic field for the benefit of the human family. (CS 62)

Teaching and learning and the interaction between teachers, support staff and pupils in a Catholic school must fully recognise 'the equality of the dignity of every human person' (CPMS 45).

The Catholic school in partnership with the wider christian community. The ecclesial dimension of the Catholic school requires partnership with the wider christian community. Such cooperation is 'a duty in conscience for all the members of the community, teachers, parents, pupils, administrative personnel' (CS 61). At a local level Catholic schools need to be part of a wider overall pastoral strategy, the undertaking of which involves 'apostolic cooperation on the part of clergy, religious and laity' (CS 72).[16] This requires an active interplay between the Catholic school and the wider believing community since the Catholic school can be 'a genuine experience of Church only if it takes its stand within the organic pastoral work of the Christian community' (CSTTM 12).

The Council emphasised that 'the right and duty of exercising the apostolate is common to all the faithful, clerical and lay, and lay people have their own proper competence in the building up of the Church' (CS 70).[17] CSTTM 13 refers to the contribution made by members of religious orders to the ecclesial character of the Catholic school. Their presence, side by side with priests and lay teachers, affords pupils 'a vivid image of the Church and makes recognition of its riches easier'.[18] The document expresses unease about the withdrawal of members of religious orders from Catholic schools as a response to declining numbers of religious and the move to new apostolates. The responsibilities of religious are also referred to in the Code of Canon Law:

> Canon 801 Religious institutes which have education as their mission are to keep faithfully to this mission and earnestly strive to devote themselves to Catholic education, providing this also through their own schools which, with the consent of the diocesan bishop, they have established.

Given that one of the sources which gives rise to questions concerning the role and mission of the Catholic school in the west is the changing pattern of the engagement of religious in such schools, it is worthwhile noting the view of the Church as expressed in its most recent documentation on the manner of their engagement. The Church encourages religious to remain active in Catholic and other schools despite their declining numbers and the attractiveness of other forms of apostolate. Religious are 'especially effective in educational activities and to offer a specific contribution to the work of other educators'.[19] By so doing they bear witness that the 'consecrated life lies in its being a sign, a memory and prophecy of the values of the Gospel' (CPMS 20). However, this does not necessarily mean that they should 'reserve exclusive tasks for themselves' in schools (CPMS 20). Their role is to 'bear witness to authentic values' (CPMS 75) and, rather than focusing on academic prestige, they should ensure that the school fosters 'the human and Christian maturation of the young people' (CPMS 75). The lived experience of the religiously professed in being part of a religious community enables them to make a unique contribution to the school as a true ecclesial community by witnessing to the 'overcoming individualistic self-promotion, solidarity instead of competition, assisting the weak instead of marginalisation, responsible participation instead of indifference' (CPMS 46). This involves a close partnership between the lay staff and the religiously professed in the school. 'To discharge this responsibility they must be careful not to get involved exclusively in academic-administrative tasks and to not be taken over by activism. What they must do is favour attention to the richness of their charism and try to develop it in response to the new social-cultural situations' (CPMS 57). There are many who would argue that this is precisely the challenge facing school leadership in the Irish Catholic school context.

The principle of lay involvement in Catholic schools is well established, the Church 'is willing to give lay people charge of the schools that it has established, and the laity themselves establish schools' (RDECS 38). However, the Church believes that 'both Religious and Lay Catholics are needed in schools' (LCS 3).

Characteristic 3: The Cultural Identity of the Catholic School

CSTTM 14 addresses the third distinctive attribute of the Catholic school: to promote a 'synthesis between culture and

161

faith'. As an ecclesial entity the Catholic school shares in the wider educational activity of the Church by which 'faith, culture and life are brought into harmony' (CS 34). Reflections on the nature of culture, and dialogue with culture as the primary focus of evangelisation, are central to the Church's statements during the pontificate of John Paul II. The recent document on *Consecrated Persons and their Mission in Schools* uses the evocative phrase of 'the bread of culture' and refers to culture as 'a fundamental condition for people to completely fulfil themselves, achieve a level of life that conforms to their dignity and open themselves to encounter with Christ and the Gospel' (CPMS 30). *The Catholic School* too called for a synthesis between faith and culture, and faith and life. The task of the Catholic school is fundamentally one of synthesis:

> a synthesis of culture and faith, and a synthesis of faith and life: the first is reached by integrating all the different aspects of human knowledge through the subjects taught, in the light of the Gospel; the second in the growth of the virtues characteristic of the Christian. (CS 37)

> The specific mission of the school, then, is a critical, systematic transmission of culture in the light of faith and the bringing forth of the power of Christian virtue by the integration of culture with faith and of faith with living. (CS 49)

Such a synthesis is central to the educational philosophy of a Catholic school (RDECS 34). By proclaiming the Gospel in the context of 'the cultural conditions of the times' (CS 9) the Catholic school 'finds its definition' (CS 9).

Inculturation: promoting a dialogue between faith and culture. The Second Vatican Council saw the Gospel as renewing and purifying human culture. *Gaudium et spes* 58 stated that:

162

God has spoken to humanity according to the culture proper to each age. Similarly the Church, which in the course of time has existed in varying circumstances, has used the resources of different cultures in her preaching to spread and explain the message of Christ.

The document continued to state that:

the Church, sent to all peoples of every time and place, is not bound exclusively and indissolubly to any race or nation, any particular way of life or any customary way of life recent or ancient ... She can enter into communion with the various cultures, to their enrichment and the enrichment of the Church herself.

The Council highlighted that the Church's duty to evangelise demands that it seeks to be in dialogue with the contemporary world in particular faith and culture and faith and science must be in dialogue. This theme has been developed continuously since the Council. In 1975 Paul VI noted:

what matters is to evangelise man's culture and cultures ... (in a vital way, in depth and right to their very roots) ... always taking the person as one's starting-point and always coming back to the relationships of people among themselves and with God. The split between the Gospel and culture is without a doubt the drama of our time ... every effort must be made to ensure a full evangelisation of culture. (EN 20)

Such dialogue is two-way; it enriches both the Church and culture since 'the Church has progressively used the sources and the means of culture in order to deepen her understanding of revelation and promote constructive dialogue with the world'

(CS 10). 'While faith is not to be identified with any one culture and is independent of all cultures, it must inspire every culture' (RDECS 53). Not only does the Church influence culture and is, in turn, conditioned by culture, 'the Church embraces everything in human culture which is compatible with Revelation ... the close relationship between culture and the life of the Church is an especially clear manifestation of the unity that exists between creation and redemption' (LCS 20). One of the initiatives of the present pope was the establishment in 1982 of the Pontifical Council for Culture. The first use of the term 'inculturation' by a pope in official documentation was by John Paul II in *Catechesi tradendae* in which he stated that:

> Catechesis ... is called to bring the power of the Gospel into the very heart of culture and cultures ... Catechesis will seek to know these cultures and their essential components; it will learn their most significant expressions; it will respect their particular values and riches ... The power of the Gospel everywhere transforms and regenerates. When that power enters into a culture, it is no surprise that it rectifies many of its elements. (CT 53)

A synthesis within the human person. Such a dialogue is essential if the Catholic school is to contribute to 'the total formation of man' (CS 15). The school is 'a privileged place in which, through a living encounter with a cultural inheritance, integral formation occurs' (CS 26). The synthesis between faith and culture is primarily to occur within each human person, specifically within each pupil. 'The world of human culture and the world of religion are not like two parallel lines that never meet; points of contact are established within the human person. For a believer is both human and a person of faith, the protagonist of culture and the subject of religion' (RDECS 51). Indeed 'culture must correspond to the human person' (CPMS 60). The challenges that human culture poses for belief lead to 'a mature faith' (RDECS 52). The comment of John Paul II taken from his letter establishing the Pontifical Council for Culture in 1982 is often quoted: 'faith which does not become culture is faith which is not received fully, not assimilated entirely, not lived faithfully.'

Virtue and character, the integration of faith and life. The second area requiring a personal synthesis is that between faith and life. This is increasingly difficult 'because of the inadequacy of the family and society' (CS 45). Further, such a synthesis is 'a life-long process of conversion' which is not limited to or completed during the period of formal schooling. Values are not just learned in the formal period of religious education but 'are cultivated in all subject areas and, indeed, in all of the various activities going on in the school' (RDECS 10). In response to cultural pluralism the Catholic school needs to provide 'strong character formation' for its pupils (CS 12).

Cultural discernment, analysis and transformation. Education requires cultural discernment as well as cultural assimilation:

> Culture is only educational when young people can relate their study to real-life situations with which they are familiar. The school must stimulate the pupil to exercise his intelligence through the dynamics of understanding to attain clarity and inventiveness. It must help him spell out the meaning of his experiences and their truths. Any school which neglects this duty and which offers merely pre-cast conclusions hinders the personal development of its pupils. (CS 27)

Gaudium et spes (59) notes that 'culture is to be subordinated to the integral perfection of the human person, to the good of the community and of the whole society. Therefore, it is necessary to develop the human faculties in such a way that there results a growth of the faculty of admiration, of intuition, of contemplation, of making personal judgement, of developing a religious, moral and social sense'. The Gospel of Jesus is thus offered as a means of cultural analysis and discernment since 'it is Christian thought which constitutes a sound criterion of judgement in the midst of conflicting concepts and behaviour ... reference to Jesus Christ teaches man to discern the values which ennoble from those which degrade him' (CS 11).[20] The dialogue with culture must therefore be 'critical and evaluative, historical and dynamic' (LCS 20) and involves raising questions about 'the fundamental ethical trends that characterise the cultural experiences of a particular community' (CPMS 68). Indeed, 'Cultures, like the people who give rise to them, are marked by the "mystery of evil" at work in human history (cf. 1Th 2:7), and they too are in need of purification and salvation. The authenticity of each human culture, the soundness of its underlying *ethos*, and hence the validity of its moral bearings, can be measured to an extent by its commitment to the human cause and by its capacity to promote human dignity at every level and in every circumstance'.[21]

Intercultural dialogue. In most western countries the education provided by Catholic Schools does not occur within a mono-cultural environment. Globalisation has been one of the major effects of market capitalism and the communications revolution and has been particularly evident in the migration of people from one country to another. How to respond to the phenomenon of multi-culturalism poses challenges for Catholic schools. The Church sees 'cultural differences as a richness' and invites schools to promote among their pupils 'an intercultural vision' (CPMS 65). It is not sufficient to simply promote tolerance of other cultures; what is required is a cherishing of difference, a 'welcome and a search for reasons for mutual understanding to intercultural dialogue, which leads to acknowledging the values and limits of every culture' (CPMS 65). John Paul II[22] has stressed 'various

166

cultures are in actual fact just different ways of dealing with the question of the meaning of personal existence. In fact, every culture is an attempt to reflect on the mystery of the world and of man, a way of expressing the transcendent dimension of human life'. Thus, cultural difference rather than being seen as a threat, 'can become, through respectful dialogue, a source of deep understanding of the mystery of human existence' (CPMS 68). Indeed, 'education leads to a realisation of the inherent limits in one's own culture and in that of others' (CPMS 79) and 'education is the main road to peace', a peace flowing 'from the heart' (CPMS 78) between peoples and cultures.

School-based religious education. A consideration of religious education could really be related to any of the six attributes of the Catholic school. We shall consider it here simply because of the cultural context in which both religious education and the school work. In so doing we are following *Catechesi tradendae* 69, which notes, 'the special character of the Catholic school and the underlying reason for its existence, the reason why Catholic parents should prefer it, is precisely the quality of the religious instruction integrated into the overall education of the students'.

Such religious education is offered to all pupils, Catholic and non-Catholic, as a 'cultural proposal' (CPMS 54). In many contexts (including the Irish context) Christianity already forms the spiritual *horizon* of the native culture. The scope of the teaching of religion in a Catholic school is broader than that in other schools, being 'that of opening (its students) to the understanding of the historical experience of Christianity, of guiding to knowledge of Jesus Christ and the study of his Gospel' (CPMS 54). The teaching of religion must 'help students to arrive at a personal position in religious matters that is consistent and respectful of the positions of others, so contributing to their growth and to a more complete understanding of reality' (CPMS 54). Such formal classroom-based religious education must be accompanied by other moments and ways for educating for 'a harmony between faith and culture, faith and life' (CS 37–48). This can be seen to involve sacramental preparation, participation in communal acts of worship, prayer, involvement in the local parish community and social action at local, national and international levels.

Catechesis, religious education. The Church in her documentation repeatedly recognises that there is both a distinction and a connection between catechesis and religious education. GE 4 considers catechesis as a broader activity distinct from, but related to, the work of moral and religious education that should be found in all schools. It considers that 'the proper place for catechesis is the family helped by other Christian communities, especially the local parish' (CS 51). 'The fundamental difference between religious and other forms of education is that its aim is not simply intellectual assent to religious truths but also a total commitment of one's whole being to the person of Christ' (CS 50). Thus, the school too has a role in catechesis to help young people 'grow towards maturity in faith' (CS 51):

> There is a close connection, and at the same time a clear distinction, between religious instruction and catechesis or the handing on of the Gospel message. The close connection makes it possible for a school to remain a school and still integrate culture with the message of Christianity. The distinction comes from the fact that, unlike religious instruction, catechesis presupposes that the hearer is receiving the Christian message as a salvific reality. Moreover, catechesis takes place within a community living out its faith at a level of space and time not available to a school: a whole lifetime. (RDECS 68)

The aim of catechesis, or handing on the Gospel message, is maturity: spiritual, liturgical, sacramental and apostolic. This happens most especially in a local Church community. The aim of the school, however, is knowledge. While it uses the same elements of the Gospel message, it tries to convey a sense of the nature of Christianity and of the hope with which Christians are trying to live their lives. It is evident, of course, that religious instruction cannot help but strengthen the faith of a believing student, just as catechesis cannot help but increase one's knowledge of the Christian message (RDECS 69).

Religious instruction in the school needs to be coordinated with the catechesis offered in parishes, in the family and in many other contexts with youth. Religious instruction, however, should be a formal part of the school curriculum and:

> should have a place in the weekly order alongside the other classes ... it should have its own syllabus, approved by those in authority; it should seek appropriate interdisciplinary links with other course materials so that there is a coordination between human learning and religious awareness. Like other course work, it should promote culture, and it should make use of the best educational methods available to schools today. In some countries, the results of examinations in religious knowledge are included within the overall measure of student progress. (RDECS 70)

Teachers of religion. 'The religion teacher is the key, the vital component, if the educational goals of the school are to be achieved' (RDECS 96). GE 9 calls for the establishment of institutes for 'preparing teachers for religious instruction'. There is a need for 'the best possible qualified teachers of religion' (CS 52). They must have a thorough cultural, professional and pedagogical training, and they must be capable of 'genuine dialogue' (RDECS 97). An 'unprepared teacher can do a great deal of harm'.

The appointment and removal of teachers of religion in Catholic schools is also referred to in the Code of Canon Law:

> Canon 804 §2 The local Ordinary is to be careful that those who are appointed as teachers of religion in schools, even non-Catholic ones, are outstanding in true doctrine, in the witness of their Christian life, and in their teaching ability.
>
> Canon 805 In his own diocese, the local Ordinary has the right to appoint or to approve teachers of religion and, if religious or moral considerations require it, the right to remove them or to demand that they be removed.

The Church describes the teaching of religion itself, by both the religious professed and lay people, as an act of personalised accompaniment involving above all else dialogue and attentive listening to both individual pupils and the wider society since 'education is a thing of the heart'[23] and 'an authentic formative process can only be initiated through a personal relationship' (CPMS 62). Such dialogue is intended to lead to the reawaking on the part of the pupil of 'the desire for internal liberation' since 'every human being feels that he is internally oppressed by tendencies to evil, even when he flaunts limitless freedom' (CPMS 63).

Chaplains and pastoral care. In GE 10 the seed can be seen for the development of what subsequently became known as Chaplains and Lay Coordinators of Chaplaincy in the educational sector: 'priests, religious and laity, carefully selected and prepared, should give abiding spiritual and intellectual assistance to the youth of the university.' In later documents this is extended to school pupils: 'the ideal would be for each student to have an opportunity for spiritual guidance, to help in interior formation. It is the best way of giving orientation and completion to the religious instruction given in the classroom and, at the same time, of integrating this instruction into the personal experiences of each individual' (RDECS 95). CS 78 refers to the need for pastoral care of teachers as well as pupils.

An integrated curriculum. The synthesis between faith and culture and between faith and life requires what has been called the 'integrated curriculum' that is to find expression in all aspects of the life of the school. This requires commitment and conviction on the part of all teachers since 'all subjects collaborate, each with its own specific content, to the formation of mature personalities' (CS 39):

> The endeavour to interweave reason and faith, which has become the heart of individual subjects, makes for unity, articulation and coordination, bringing forth within what is learnt in school a Christian vision of the world, of life, of culture and of history. In the Catholic school's educational project there is no separation between time for learning and time for formation, between acquiring notions and growing in wisdom. The various school subjects do not present only knowledge to be attained, but also values to be acquired and truths to be discovered. (CS 39)

Thus, the teaching of all subjects, not just religious education, must highlight 'the humanistic and spiritual dimension of knowledge' (CPMS 39).

Characteristic 4: Education as a Work of Loving Care

We turn now to the fourth characteristic of the Catholic school identified in the *Catholic School on the Threshold of the Third Millennium*: education as a work of loving care. In the Irish context this can be seen as referring to general school ethos and a preferential option for the poor in society. Much has already been said concerning general ethos; the school should be primarily experienced by pupils as a community rather than as an institution, it should focus upon the full human development of each individual pupil and it should be characterised by the Gospel values of freedom, justice and love. At all times it should take Christ as its centre and invite all who form part of its community to conversion of heart and to discipleship.

A preferential option for the poor. Not only must the Catholic school be a community, it must be an inclusive community with a special concern for the weakest in society. GE 9 first highlighted the preferential option that Catholic schools should make for both the materially and spiritually poor. The school should care especially for 'those who are poor in the goods of this world or who are deprived of the assistance and affection of a family or who are strangers to the gift of faith'. This wording has been repeated in subsequent documentation, for instance CS 58 insists that first and foremost the Church offers its educational service to 'the poor or those who are deprived of family help and affection or those who are far from the faith'. If the Catholic school were to turn its attention exclusively or predominantly to those from the wealthier social classes, 'it could be contributing towards maintaining their privileged position, and could thereby continue to favour a society which is unjust' (CS 58). CSTTM 15 again repeats this concern for the weakest in society including the 'new poor', 'those who have lost all sense of meaning in life and lack any type of inspiring ideal, those to whom no values are proposed and who do not know the beauty of faith, who come from families which are broken and incapable of love, often living in situations of material and spiritual poverty, slaves to the new idols of a society, which, not infrequently, promises them only a future of unemployment and marginalisation'.

A preferential option for the poor requires a commitment to 'start from the least' and 'give a voice to the poor' (CPMS

69–72). The Catholic school must avoid all forms of exclusion. This requires 'a transformation of the logics of excellence and superiority into those of service, of *caring for others* and forming a heart that is open to solidarity' (CPMS 69) and a commitment to ensure that 'the best resources and most qualified persons are initially placed at the service of the least, without in this way excluding those who have less difficulties and shortages' (CPMS 70). Such a stance can be seen as part of what is often referred to as the 'hidden curriculum' by which a school teaches not only by what it says but also by what it does. The school is invited to listen 'to the poorest people' and 'arrange itself to suit them'; by so doing it contributes to 'the global growth of people' (CPMS 72). Becoming the voice of the poor of the world[24] is 'a challenge assumed by the Church' and all Christians, including the teachers and pupils in the school, 'should do the same'.

Characteristic 5: The Catholic School at the Service of Society

Education for citizenship. The Catholic school must be inserted into the local society of which it forms a part; it has a public role as well as an ecclesial role. CSTTM 16 states that the Catholic school 'cannot be considered separately from other educational institutions and administered as an entity apart, but must be related to the world of politics, economy, culture and society as a whole'. The Catholic school should promote the values of citizenship and human solidarity. 'A Christian education must promote respect for the state and its representatives, the observance of just laws and a search for the common good. Therefore, traditional civic values such as freedom, justice, the nobility of work and the need to pursue social progress are all included among the school goals ...' (RDECS 45).

Such education for citizenship should not be restricted to a narrow national focus but should promote 'responsible participation in the life of the community at local, national and world levels' (CPMS 80). Citizenship requires a global awareness and ethic:

> Among the challenges of modern society that schools have to face are threats to life and to families, genetic manipulations, growing pollution, plundering of natural resources, the unsolved drama of the underdevelopment and poverty that crush entire populations of the south of the world. These are vital questions for everyone, which need to be faced with extensive and responsible vision, promoting a concept of life that respects the dignity of man and of creation. This means forming persons who are able to dominate and transform processes and instruments in a sense that is humanizing and filled with solidarity. (CPMS 34)[25]

The Catholic school as a community actively working for justice. The Catholic school should be both itself experienced as a just community and, as a community, work for justice in human society. 'The Catholic school is particularly sensitive to the call from every part of the world for a more just society, and it tries to make its own contribution towards it. It ... tries to put these demands into practice in its own community in the daily life of the school' (CS 58). It must also promote an awareness of justice in international society, seeing all of humanity as one large family and working for 'peace, justice, freedom, progress for all peoples and assistance for countries in need' (RDECS 45). Ongoing social development is a key aim of the Catholic school. Catholic teachers should develop in themselves and their pupils 'a keen social awareness and a profound sense of civic and political responsibility. ... [They should form] men and women who will make the "civilization of love" a reality' (LCS 19).

A deep respect for knowledge. The Catholic school should also promote 'a deep awareness of the value of knowledge as such' (CS 38). In the teaching of all subjects on the curriculum the aim is 'not merely the attainment of knowledge but the acquisition of values and the discovery of truth' (CS 39). Through study and research the pupil 'contributes to perfecting himself and his humanity. Study becomes the path for a personal encounter with the truth, a "place" of encounter with God himself. Taken this way, knowledge can help to motivate existence, to begin the search for God, it can be a great experience of freedom for truth, placing itself in the service of the maturation and promotion of humanity' (CPMS 39).[26] The importance of academic standards is also referred to in the Code of Canon Law:

> Canon 806 §2 Those who are in charge of Catholic schools are to ensure, under the supervision of the local Ordinary, that the formation given in them is, in its academic standards, at least as outstanding as that in other schools in the area.

A welcome for non-Catholic pupils. The Vatican Council highlighted not just individual religious freedom but the importance of ecumenical and inter-religious dialogue. In its subsequent documentation, the Church repeatedly acknowledges the presence of non-Catholics (other Christians, members of non-Christian faiths and non-believers) within its own schools. Admission to a Catholic school should not be reserved to Catholics only, but be open to 'all those who appreciate' its work. It should promote 'civil progress and human development without discrimination of any kind' (GE 9). The school should promote cooperation and contact between different belief systems and must open 'itself to others and [respect] their way of thinking and of living'. The Catholic school must 'share their anxieties and their hopes as it, indeed, shares their present and future lot in this world' (CS 57).

Religious freedom and freedom of conscience. RDECS 6 seeks to balance individual religious freedom and freedom of conscience with the duty of the school to be an agent of evangelisation:

> The religious freedom and the personal conscience of individual students and their families must be respected and this freedom is explicitly recognised by the Church.[27] On the other hand, a Catholic school cannot relinquish its own freedom to proclaim the Gospel and to offer a formation based on the values to be found in a Christian education; this is its right and its duty. To proclaim or to offer is not to impose, however; the latter suggests a moral violence which is strictly forbidden, both by the Gospel and by Church law.[28]

'An encounter with God is always a personal event, an answer that is by its nature a person's free act in response to the gift of faith' (CPMS 5). Thus, when educating pupils from non-Christian faiths the Catholic school should be 'especially attentive to the practical effects of [their] culture and strengthen those aspects of it which will make a person more human. In particular, it ought to pay attention to the religious dimension of the culture and to the emerging ethical requirements to be found in it' (RDECS 108). It must acknowledge 'the freedom and right of families to see that their children receive the sort of education they wish for them'[29] and acknowledge the right of each person to receive a suitable education of their free choice (CSTTM 17).

In approaching religious education with pupils of other faiths and none, the emphasis should be upon the 'search for meaning' (CPMS 51). While a Catholic school does not demand adherence to the faith, it can prepare for it by creating the conditions for 'a person to develop a gift for searching and to be guided in discovering the mystery of his being and of the reality that surrounds him, until he reaches the threshold of the faith' (CPMS 51). Once a person freely decides to cross this threshold he or she can be offered the necessary means 'for continuing to deepen their experience of faith through prayer, the sacraments, the encounter with Christ in the Word, in the Eucharist, in events and persons' (CPMS 51).

Cooperation with other schools. The Church acknowledges the objection that others can see a separate and distinctive Catholic school system as being socially divisive. Catholic schools therefore must not work in isolation from other schools but 'every means should be employed to foster suitable cooperation between Catholic schools, and between these and other schools that collaboration should be developed which the good of all mankind requires' (GE 12). The Catholic school should be characterised by openness, collaboration and dialogue based on 'mutual respect' and an awareness of the 'common service to mankind' (CSTTM 17). Thus, Catholic schools can work with any civil authority or state that respects 'the fundamental rights of the human person, starting with respect for life and religious freedom'.

Characteristic 6: The Climate of the Educating Community
Finally we turn our attention to the sixth dimension of education: the promotion and sustaining of the ethos or characteristic spirit of the Catholic school. Since the formation of the human person is dependant upon the quality of 'interpersonal relations', RDECS 32 and CSTTM 18 both stress that the Catholic school should involve interaction and collaboration between all members of the school community 'students, parents, teachers, directors and non-teaching staff'.[30] 'Faith is principally assimilated through contact with people whose daily life bears witness to it' (CS 53). The school must

create a community 'in which the values are mediated by authentic interpersonal relations between the various members of which it is composed' (CPMS 41).

Empowering parents as educators. The first and primary educators of children are their parents; 'the family is the first school of the social virtues that every society needs' (GE 3). RDECS 42 stresses partnership with parents, while RDECS 43 states that school must raise parents' awareness of their role. CSTTM 20 notes that today there is a widespread tendency for parents to 'delegate this unique role' to other agencies. The school must undertake initiatives 'aimed at rendering increasingly more active the insertion of parents in the life of [the school] and for making them aware of the educational task' (CPMS 47).

Teachers as educators of the whole person. 'The quality of the teachers is fundamental in creating an educational environment that is purposeful and fertile' (CPMS 59). GE outlines the role of the teacher in the Catholic school on whom the school depends 'almost entirely for the accomplishment of its goals and programmes' (GE 8). 'By their witness and their behaviour teachers are of the first importance to impart a distinctive character to Catholic schools' (CS 78). The work of teachers 'is in the real sense of the word an apostolate most suited to and necessary for our times and at once a true service offered to society'(GE 8). While every person who contributes to integral human formation is an educator, 'teachers have made integral human formation their very profession' (LCS 15). The 'teacher' is to be understood as an 'educator', 'one who helps to form human persons. The task of a teacher goes well beyond the transmission of knowledge' (LCS 16). To lay teachers in particular, as members of the Church community, 'the family and the Church entrust the school's educational endeavour' (LCS 24). Teachers should be 'intimately linked in charity to one another and to their students', 'bear witness to Christ' by their life as much as by their instruction, and work 'as partners with parents' (GE 8). Teachers are encouraged 'to persevere generously in the work they have undertaken and, imbuing their students with the spirit of Christ, to strive to excel in pedagogy and the pursuit of knowledge in such a way that they not merely advance the internal renewal of the Church but preserve and enhance its beneficent influence upon today's world, especially the intellectual world' (GE, conclusion). CSTTM 19 invites teachers to see teaching as an ethical activity: 'teaching has an extraordinary moral depth and is one of man's most excellent and creative activities, for the teacher does not write on inanimate material, but on the very spirits of human beings.' Teaching therefore has both a professional and a vocational dimension (LCSWF 24 and CPMS 59).

The mandate to teach. The Catholic School refers to 'teachers' and adults' authority' to educate (CS 29). 'Catholic teachers who freely accept posts in schools, which have a distinctive character, are obliged to respect that character and give their active support to it under the direction of those responsible' (CS 80). The need for a balance between respect for individual freedom and a shared 'unity of purpose'. 'It is obvious that in such a demanding educational policy all participants must be committed to it freely. It cannot be imposed, but is offered as a possibility, as good news, and as such can be refused. However, in order to bring it into being and to maintain it, the school must be able to count on the unity of purpose and conviction of all its members' (CS 59).

CONCLUSION: THE EMBEDDED NATURE OF CATHOLIC SCHOOLS IN IRELAND

The above reflections on the theological basis of Catholic schools in Ireland clearly focus the central question of the nature and purpose of such schools. This is an urgent question that in general should be answered by reference to the six religious dimensions of education discussed above. However, any specific approaches to implementing these general dimensions for Catholic schools in Ireland must move from seeing such schools as isolated entities or institutions to seeing them as embedded communities, the nature and purpose of which depend upon a clear understanding of other linked factors and contexts. Catholic schools are embedded in a wider ecclesial framework which seeks to serve the Church's mission of evangelisation at the start of the third millennium; they are embedded in a partnership framework with parents, teachers and other social partners (as reflected in the 1998 Education Act); and they are embedded within a wider constitutional, legal, economic and socio-cultural framework. The shape of these wider frameworks determine the specific identity and purpose of Catholic schools in Ireland with the broad umbrella of the above six religious dimensions of education.

At this stage it is also important to voice a word of caution. The Church's documentation on schooling often presumes a distinction between Church and State that finds expression in a parallel system of secular state schools and church-related faith schools. This is not the case in Ireland, which has a denominationally based system of schooling provided for, rather than provided by, the State. Thus, all schools at primary level can be regarded as faith schools being either denominational or multi-denominational in character. At second level a similar position can be argued: schools are either denominational (voluntary secondary schools) or multi-denominational (community and comprehensive schools or vocational schools and community colleges). Multi-denominational schools, the majority of pupils of which are Catholic, cannot be regarded as State schools in the normally accepted understanding of that term. To over-emphasise the catholicity of Catholic denominational schools runs the risk of ignoring the religious dimension of education for Catholic and other pupils in multi-denominational contexts. Our concern must be with the religious dimension of schooling for all pupils, the majority of whom are baptised into the Catholic faith, in whatever school context they find themselves.

The first layer of embeddedment for schools is the wider ecclesial context of a partnership between the family, the parish and the school as the three agencies of religious formation. In the Irish context it is increasingly apparent that the school provides many pupils with their most significant experience of the community of faith. The mission of the Church to evangelise by education requires a clear definition of the role and inter-connectedness of each of these agencies in life-long and ongoing religious formation. In the absence of a clearly articulated pastoral plan for evangelisation by the Catholic Church in Ireland it is difficult to see how Catholic schools and church-related schools can specify their distinctive purpose and role.

In this context it is clear that too tight a distinction between school-based catechesis and school-based religious education is of little use in the Irish context since it presumes a dual education system (State schools and Catholic schools) with a clear and real choice available to parents, pupils and teachers between a Church schooling system and a State schooling system. Such a distinction does not exist in the Republic of Ireland (although it does in Northern Ireland as part of the United Kingdom). It is more useful to distinguish between school-based religious education and parish or home-based catechesis as distinct but connected approaches. Given the intimate relationship between the local community, the local school and the local parish that remains evident especially in rural Ireland, most of the work of religious education still rests on the school (although this may quickly change given current unease about sacramental preparation within primary schools). Thus, in practice the real issue is between religious education and other faith-development initiatives. And within school-based religious education, the issue is how to nurture faith in a manner that is educationally justifiable within an increasingly ecumenical and inter-faith environment and given a growing apathy towards institutionalised religion. Thus, school-based religious education should neither ignore faith nor presume faith: it should acknowledge faith as a key learning resource.

The second layer of embeddedment for schools is that of social partnership, particularly with parents and teachers. The primary responsibility for education rests with the parents of the child who come together with others (in this case the Patron of the school) to provide for the education of their child. As is the case with many western countries, Ireland faces a particular challenge in empowering parents in their role as educators. As the curriculum at second level becomes more and more specialised, parents are increasingly marginalised; even many parents with a strong personal faith commitment feel inadequate to contribute to the religious formation of their children. Although parents have representation on the Board of Management of most primary and second-level schools, in practice their role is often limited to pragmatic tasks such as fund-raising. While there have been some initiatives to raise the consciousness of parents of their role, much more needs to be done. Further, there is insufficient evidence that parents choose the Catholic school because of the religious dimension of the education it provides. Often the school is chosen because it is the local school or because of its academic profile. Parents in Ireland not only need to be empowered to act as active partners in education generally but to provide for the religious formation of their children in partnership with the school and the wider parish. If the religious education of the child through the school is isolated from the wider religious, moral and spiritual formation provided by the home then little can be really achieved.

Similarly, the school acts in partnership with the teachers employed by the managers of the school. This area too is problematic both for school leaders (principals, deputy principals, year heads etc.) and general subject teachers. The issue of leadership succession is a real issue in Irish schools. As the religiously professed vacate positions of leadership to be replaced with lay principals and lay boards of management, the transmission of the charism and characteristic spirit of Catholic schools from one generation of leaders to the next assumes considerable urgency. What was taken for granted in the past cannot be taken for granted in the present or in the future. Those assuming positions of leadership need ongoing formation and support in the specific educational vision of the religious dimension of Catholic education and schooling.

Clearly the school principal has a pivotal role in giving effect to the six attributes of the religious dimension of education in the Catholic school. In some countries, for example Australia and New Zealand, the school principal has a contractual obligation to uphold and promote the distinctive ethos of the Catholic school, and is invited to see themselves as a religious leader. Such a formal contract relationship does not yet apply in the Irish context and would be premature. However, it is certain that much needs to be done to support lay men and women in the principal's role of school leader with respect to the characteristic spirit of both voluntary Catholic secondary schools, vocational community colleges and community schools.

The same applies to all teachers in the school community. There is a growing recognition in the Irish context of the need to promote staff awareness of characteristic spirit. It is generally recognised that schooling in Ireland is very successful and has contributed in a substantive manner to recent rapid economic expansion. Teachers in general are regarded as competent and committed to their work. However, given the absence of separate Church and State schooling systems it would be unreasonable to impose too rigorous a set of demands upon teachers concerning personal religious commitment. In general, teachers in the Irish context make a decision to teach;

unless they are working within the areas of religious education and chaplaincy they do not necessarily make the decision to teach within a school which defines itself as an 'ecclesial community'.

Teaching and learning can be viewed as an interaction between persons, the teacher and the pupil, within the context of a body of content, the curriculum. A significant development within the Irish second-level curriculum is the introduction of a state syllabus for religious education initially at Junior Certificate level and eventually at Leaving Certificate level. This syllabus describes itself as ecumenical and inter-faith but can be adapted at local level to suit the needs of the characteristic spirit of a specific school. The new syllabus is, however, raising significant questions concerning the balance between religious knowledge and understanding on the one hand and faith formation and human development on the other hand.

In addition, the ideal of an Integrated Curriculum in Catholic schools poses real challenges in the Irish context. There are a number of issues here. Firstly extensive effort has been made in the development of religious education but in practice this is often experienced as an isolated area of the curriculum. Secondly, each diocese appoints a diocesan advisor for religious education at both primary and secondary level. However, the work of such advisors is restricted to the area of religious education and does not extend to the religious dimension of all curriculum areas as envisaged by the notion of the integrated curriculum. Further, the advisory role of such diocesan advisors within the new state syllabus for religious education is contentious, the State seeing the role as being proper to the Department of Education Inspectorate for the new syllabus. Thirdly, the issue is further complicated by the exercise of the parental right to withdraw the pupil from religious education. While it is possible to withdraw a pupil from a timetabled period of religious education it is not of course possible to withdraw from the religious dimension of an integrated curriculum. Fourthly, teachers of general curriculum subjects are neither formally employed nor trained to explore the religious dimension of such subjects. In Ireland there has been no real formal, systematic or sustained exploration of the implications of the integrated curriculum such as is evident in the Australian Catholic Archdiocese of Sydney's *Sense of the Sacred* initiative. Some signs of openness to such a development are evident in the Irish context within the RSE programme.

Finally, the school is embedded in a socio-cultural context. As religious belief is marginalised and individualised by the rise of secularism, the work of the school in sustaining or enhancing the religious dimension of education becomes more difficult. Religious commitment is not just a matter of private personal belief but involves a radical commitment to the other, the other in human society at personal, local, national and international levels, and the Ultimate Other whom Christians name as the Father of Jesus Christ. The sense of transcendence is being dulled in contemporary Irish society and as this happens the wellsprings of spirituality dry up.

The fundamental option for the education of the poor is also a vital question for Catholic schooling in Ireland. Historically, religious congregations (often founded explicitly for the education of the poor) ran Catholic voluntary secondary schools. Free second-level education was only introduced into Ireland in 1966 and, in practice, in the mid-twentieth century such religiously run schools began to attract the children of parents who could afford to pay the admittedly modest fees. Such schools tended to be single sexed and offered an academic education that enhanced the entry of its school leavers into the civil and public service and into third-level education (also fee paying). The State established a parallel system of non-denominational vocational schools that largely developed skills for the workplace. In recent years a newer form of second-level school has emerged, the community school, which offers a holistic curriculum and is co-educational. All new schools are community schools and many former religious-run single-sex Catholic secondary schools are merging in the context of community schools. Thus, distinctively Catholic secondary schools are often perceived in elitist terms. The 'new poor' as described in the Church's documentation on education are more often to be found in the community and vocational school sectors.

As Irish society becomes less religiously literate, one can no longer presume a level of faith commitment on the part of pupils, teachers or parents. Given the fact that the Republic has a Church-linked system of education with no substantive state schooling sector, it would be unreasonable to presume that all who work within the school, or that all who attend the school, would have a strong faith commitment. It is vital, however, that the school remain a community that is hospitable to faith and in which the sacred and the secular are not divorced from each other. Such a development would deny the incarnational theology on which the Catholic view of education and schooling is based.

Schools must increasingly offer an invitation to faith rather than presuming that such faith is already present. This invitation is primarily one to faith in Jesus and to a response of discipleship. It is Christ that the school must proclaim; it is a personal relationship with God in Christ that it must offer. In so doing it will be a school for human persons, of human persons. It is Jesus who reveals the fullness of what it is to be human; it is he who guides our search for meaning. It is through conversion to him that the individual and wider Irish culture can be transformed. This is the hope of John Paul II at the start of the third millennium:

'Your face, O Lord, I seek' (Ps 27:8). The ancient longing of the Psalmist could receive no fulfilment greater and more surprising than the contemplation of the face of Christ. God has truly blessed us in him and has made 'his

186

face to shine upon us' (Ps 67:1). At the same time, God and man that he is, he reveals to us also the true face of man, 'fully revealing man to man himself' ... Jesus is 'the new man' (cf. Eph 4:24; Col 3:10) who calls redeemed humanity to share in his divine life. The mystery of the Incarnation lays the foundations for an anthropology which, reaching beyond its own limitations and contradictions, moves towards God himself, indeed towards the goal of 'divinization' (*Novo millennio ineunte* (2000) par. 23).

'[Evangelisation] has its centre in Christ himself, who is to be known, loved and imitated, so that in him we may live the life of the Trinity, and with him transform history until its fulfilment in the heavenly Jerusalem'. *Novo millennio ineunte* (2000) par. 29

Notes

1   For convenience the following abbreviations will be used in this paper:
GE: *Gravissimum educationis;* LG: *Lumen gentium;* DV: *Dei Verbum;* AA: *Apostolicam actuositatem;* CT: *Catechesi tradendae;* FR: *Fides et ratio;* CS: The Catholic School; LCS: Lay Catholics in Schools: Witnesses to the Faith; RDECS: The Religious Dimension of Education in the Catholic School; CSTTM: Catholic School on the Threshold of the Third Millennium; CCC: The Catechism of the Catholic Church; GFFDCS: Guidelines for the Faith Formation and Development of Catholic Students; CPMS: Consecrated Persons and their Mission in Schools.

2   Irish Catholic Bishops' Conference, *A Syllabus for the Religious Education of Catholic Pupils in Post-Primary Schools* (1982), p. 4.

3   Irish Catholic Bishops' Conference, *Guidelines for the Faith Formation and Development of Catholic Students*, Dublin: Veritas, 1999, p. 5.

4   M. Kennedy, *Islands Apart*, Dublin: Veritas, 2000, p. 3.

5   Dermot Lane, *Catholic Education and the School: Some Theological Reflections*, Dublin: Veritas, 1991, pp. 4–5.

6   *Gravissimum educationis*, n. 8.

7   Reported in 2 ILRM (1998).

8   CPSMA, revised 2000, p. 16.

9   Cf. John Paul II, 'Address to the National Meeting of the Catholic School in Italy', in *L'Osservatore Romano*, 24 November 1991, p. 4.

10   *The Catholic School*, n. 35.

11   John Paul II, Encyclical Letter, *Redemptor hominis*, n. 14.

12   Cf. *Gaudium et spes*, nn. 12; 14; 17; 22

13   Quoting John Paul II, *Jubilee of University Professors*, Rome, 9 September 2000, nn. 3, 6, *AAS* 92 (2000), pp. 863–5.

14   *Gravissimum educationis*, n. 8.

15   Irish Catholic Bishops' Conference, *Guidelines for the Faith Formation and Development of Catholic Students* (1999), p. 7.

16   *Apostolicam actuositatem*, n. 23.

17   *Apostolicam actuositatem*, n. 25.

18   John Paul II, Apostolic Exhortation, *Christifideles laici*, n. 62.

19   John Paul II, Apostolic Exhortation, *Vita consecrata*, n. 97, *AAS* 88 (1996), 473.

20   Paul VI, 'Allocution to the Ninth Congress of the Catholic International Education Office (O.I.E.C.)', in *L'Osservatore Romano*, 9 June 1974.

21   John Paul II, *Dialogue between Cultures for a Civilization of Love and Peace*, Message for the Celebration of the World Day of Peace, 1 January 2001, n. 10, *AAS* 93 (2001), 238.

22   John Paul II, *Insegnamenti*, XVIII / 2, 1995, pp. 730–4.

23   St John Bosco, *Circolare del 24 gennaio 1883*, in CERIA E. (*a cura di*), *Epistolario di S. Giovanni Bosco*, SEI, Torino 1959, Vol. IV, 209.

24   John Paul II, Apostolic Letter, *Tertio millennio adveniente*, 10 November 1994, n. 51, *AAS* 87 (1995), p. 36.

25   Quoting John Paul II, Apostolic Exhortation, *Vita Consecrata*, n. 62, *AAS* 88 (1996), p. 437.

26   Quoting John Paul II, *Speech to the Plenary Session of the Pontifical Academy of Sciences*, 13 November 2000, *AAS* 93 (2001), pp. 202–6.

27   Cf. *Dignitatis humanae*, 2; 9; 10; 12 *et passim*.

28   Code of Canon Law, canon 748 §2.

29   Cf. Holy See, Charter of Rights of the Family, art. 5.

30   S. Congregation for Catholic Education, *Lay Catholics in Schools: Witnesses to Faith*, n. 22.

The Catholic School, the Democratic State and Civil Society: Exploring the Tensions*

Joseph Dunne

INTRODUCTION

One might address educational issues from a Catholic viewpoint, or again one might address them from the perspective of a democratic state in a modern, pluralist society. Neither of these tasks would be easy, nor would the identification of a single standpoint, from which to consider education, eliminate scope for conflict and disagreement. For, even while sharing some fundamental commitments, Catholics can certainly find much to argue about among themselves as to what the priorities and emphases of the Church's policy on education (or the policies of different groups within the Church) ought to be. And something similar is true with respect to democratic theory and practice: there are difficult choices and perplexities that face, and divide, those who (even if there were no Catholic Church) have to decide what education at different levels ought to consist of, on what bases it ought to be

---

* This paper was first published as 'The Catholic School and Civil Society: Exploring the Tensions', in N. Brennan, ed., *The Catholic School in Contemporary Society*, Dublin: CMRS, 1991; as republished here, it incorporates some small typographical and stylistic corrections but no attempt at revision in the light of subsequent developments, not least in legislation.

made available and how it should be managed in a democratic society. It is especially daunting, however, if one is asked not to speak from either of these standpoints exclusively but, rather, to try to bring them together – to stand as it were on the ground where they meet, or overlap, or encroach on each other and to attempt to analyse the tensions that arise there. The doubly occupied zones that I'm talking about are very familiar: they are Roman Catholic schools in the Republic of Ireland.[1] And that there are real tensions with respect to them – tensions, I mean, that arise precisely from their dual nature – I take to be a matter of common experience.

In *historical* terms, there is the experience of great controversy going back at least to the foundation of the National System of Education in 1831 (but with roots of course in the sixteenth century) which one may read about – and on doing so, perhaps, be startled to discover just how much the central issues of the nineteenth century are, for all the huge changes that have taken place in the interim, still so obstinately at the centre of our contemporary agenda. There is, then, the political experience, the ongoing debates about where authority for educational decision making should lie – debates that are certain to be sharpened by the present proposal to bring forward, for the first time in the history of the state, a comprehensive Education Act. There is also, then, the *legal* and perhaps especially the *constitutional* dimension to education – a dimension that is made more difficult by the relative absence of legislation in this area as well as the paucity of test cases brought, or precedents established, through the courts. A further dimension is the *sociological* one, and especially the impact in Ireland over the past few decades of modernisation (and in particular its liberalising and secularising tendencies). And also to be taken into consideration, of course, are the changes in *educational* thinking, say over the past twenty-five years, as well as developments in *theology*, perhaps especially in ecclesiology or reflection on the nature of the church since Vatican II.

The matter before us is complex, however, not just because it ranges over so many specialised areas of discourse in which one may be aware that one lacks expert knowledge; it is all the more vexing because it is so concretely and pervasively present in the practices of teachers, pupils and parents, and because the conflicts that it brings into play are not just fought out by interest groups – out there as it were – but may also resound within oneself, stirring up uncomfortable questions about where one's ultimate allegiances and commitments lie. There are of course people who do not feel these conflicts within themselves, who – from one side or the other – can bemoan the ambiguity and unprincipled compromise that disfigure the history of this matter and can at the same time feel confident that the best solution is obvious, and could be implemented, if only one or other unenlightened party could be disabused of its prejudice or relieved of its power. What I shall attempt to do here is to expose what I take to be real predicaments in relation to Catholic schools and, in teasing out just why they are predicaments, to show that they raise deep questions for all the partners in education – State, Church, teachers, parents and pupils. I shall be concerned less with assertion than with argument and, in a sense, less with argument than with analysis. I say this because although my prejudices in favour of certain positions will certainly emerge (and, in being articulated, come to seem reasonable, I hope) my main concern is to identify and clarify basic issues and principles and to consider seriously arguments on different sides. I am aware that, in the present matter, this analytic approach is not a sufficient condition for resolving deep differences, let alone for making good practical decisions. Still, without it, we shall speak past each other in our debates and flounder in our public decisions.

THE DEMOCRATIC PURPOSES OF EDUCATION

From the viewpoint of a democratic state it might be argued that the school is centrally important because it is the reproductive agent of a democratic way of life on which the survival of the state itself ultimately depends. An essential purpose of basic schooling will be to cultivate civic virtue or a democratic character, if not a form of what, in less self-conscious times, was called patriotism. Minimally, this will involve respect for the basic institutions of the State; more ambitiously, it will mean an ability to participate together in shared practices in such a way that differences are respected and consensus is reached through deliberation and discussion. One can of course take a more jaundiced view than this: that the state need only interest itself in a passive type of socialisation; that it would be threatened by, and therefore should not encourage, the development of critical reflection in its young people; that education from its point of view is a thoroughly functional enterprise focused on ranges of knowledge and skill that are necessary to maintain and develop a technological society; and that schooling is a mechanism of social control insofar as it channels young people's energies into a ritualised competition for scarce rewards – in terms of jobs, income and status – and then legitimates the resulting inequality by allowing the claim that it (the inequality) is due to differential achievements based on individual merit rather than to deep-lying structural impediments to real equality of opportunity.

There is, I think, much truth in this jaundiced interpretation, in Ireland as in most developed societies today. But if a democratic state had a vision of education that was congruent with its own formal reality as a democracy (and this is without prejudice to the substantive policies which it might actually pursue through the democratic process) this vision would put a premium on the kind of civic virtues already mentioned: tolerance, a sense of responsibility, a willingness to modify one's private interest in the light of the public good, and a disposition to seek out and promote this good through participation in shared reflection and action. Democracy itself, in other words, might be seen as a normative concept, as holding out to a society an ideal which it may fall far short of even when its elections and parliamentary procedures and institutions of government are in place; and education at all levels, then, might be seen as the indispensable means through which a society tries to open and equip itself to meet this ideal. Now looked at in this way – a way which I am suggesting is not only compatible with but almost required by a democratic state – education would already have a strong moral dimension; and it would have this quite without reference to religion. Moreover, one might go on from here to suggest that what the State should have an interest in fostering through its schools is the students' identity precisely as citizens. Not that the State should at all try to suppress what is distinctive about different social sub-groups, be they religious, ethnic or linguistic; but what it should choose to emphasise in its *schooling* policy is not these differences but rather what is common to everyone as (potential) members of the polity; and it might be added that in any case the only satisfactory way of recognising and democratically dealing with these differences is precisely by having them fully represented within the same educational institutions so that from the beginning people might learn to respect, and live and cooperate with, people significantly different from themselves.

ARGUING FOR DENOMINATIONAL SCHOOLING

The argument I have just sketched, though directly an argument for a conception of democratic education, is also, indirectly but quite clearly, an argument for non-denominational schooling.[2] It has been implicitly rejected by, among others, traditional custodians of Catholic education in Ireland (as well as by the framers of our Constitution). The grounds for this rejection are along the following lines. The argument over-estimates the State's interest in education; in fact it allows the State to usurp the legitimate interests of parents. Parents have primary and inalienable (though not absolute) rights over their children's education, rights which also of course entail responsibilities. These rights may be recognised by the State (as they in fact are in the Constitution) but they are not granted by the State nor does their existence depend on its recognition of them. They entitle parents not only to choose the type of school to which they will send their children but also to make a claim on the State for some reasonable subvention of this school.

In pressing these rights and claims, one is rejecting the argument which concluded with an endorsement of universal non-denominationalism; but, in rejecting the conclusion, one need not reject all the premises of this argument. In fact, apologists for Catholic schools would claim that education in these schools is in itself an education for citizenship; the Christian virtues which it seeks to foster not only do not conflict with democratic virtues but actually enhance and as it were supercharge them. Nor is the value of pluralism *per se* contested. On the contrary, it is suggested that pluralism itself is best realised not within the school but rather by ensuring a plurality of schools. True diversity and the enrichment it can bring to society is best achieved by enabling the diverse groups to express fully and realise what is distinctive to each of them; and this in turn can be done only by granting to each the supportive milieu of its own schools.

While this counter-argument can be presented as a Catholic one – and it has characteristically been made by Catholic spokespersons – clearly it does not at all depend on specifically Catholic principles. The right it asserts is not a unique one based on the 'special position' of any one group but can equally be pressed on behalf of other groups; the good it appeals to is actually the *common* good – as indeed it can hardly avoid being since what is claimed is not just the State's tacit consent but its actual support through financial provision. The defence of Catholic schools so far, then, might be said to be based on democratic – indeed one might rather say liberal – principles. For its basic premise is that individual parents, rather than having a single state system foisted on them, should have the right to choose what type of school their children shall attend and that there should be an open market, as it were, to cater for the diversity of these choices. The implications of this kind of argument, however, should be faced. For from the premise 'parental rights', the conclusion 'Church control' does not necessarily follow. If parents in the past have, overwhelmingly, supported Catholic schools there is of course no guarantee that, as the effective clients, they will go on doing so. And one should acknowledge that certainly at primary level up to now the Church has benefited from an advantageous marketplace. With ownership of the site plus approximately 10 per cent of the capital cost being set by the State as a minimum condition for its support of a new school, the Church has not had many competitors. It has had the advantage of an organisational network that has been able to mobilise resources to an extent that, especially in a newly developing area – and with the State choosing to be a reactive rather than an initiating partner – could scarcely be matched by any other agency or group (at least one that might conceivably have education as a priority).

So far, then, the grounds for Catholic schools smack curiously of Lockean liberalism: they are based on a combination of freedom of choice and property-title. The ownership of property surely gives legal protections, but it is not clear what moral authority to educate it can confer. And while the freedom of parental choice does indeed provide a moral basis, it is potentially a discomfiting one; for it compels one to defer to any change in the way in which parents exercise this choice and, strictly, obliges one to be concerned that the choice be a real one – and not simply a function of the absence of a desired alternative. It is worth noting here that the Second Vatican Council's *Declaration on Religious Liberty* speaks of the 'right of parents to make a genuinely free choice of schools' and goes on to insist that '[t]he use of this freedom of choice is not to be made a reason for imposing unjust burdens on parents whether directly or indirectly'.[3] And in another document the same Council speaks of the duty of the public authority 'to see to it, out of concern for distributive justice, that public subsidies are allocated in such a way that, when selecting schools for their children, parents are genuinely free to follow their consciences'.[4] The directions in which these sentiments point, if they are taken seriously and applied in the Irish situation, is something that I shall return to later.

CATHOLIC EDUCATION AND ITS INTEGRAL CHARACTER

What, we may perhaps now ask, is the Catholic school? If ownership and the fact of parental support are in a sense extrinsic – insofar as they can come into play equally in the case of any other type of school – what are the more intrinsic grounds for Catholic schools? To deal with this basic question we need to stand back from the school (noticing as we do that there are not, for instance, Catholic post offices or restaurants – though there are indeed, for instance, Catholic hospitals) and ask first about Catholic education; and in doing this we should enter, as I have not so far done in this paper, into the Church's self-understanding in relation to its own nature and role.

The Church is a historical community which through faith in Jesus Christ understands itself, and goes on trying to understand itself better, as entrusted with the ultimately mysterious truth about human life; it is a community which, from its beginning and certainly today also, lives in a necessary tension between itself as a believing community and the wider community in which it finds itself. It is directed outwards to this wider community and yet also concerned to build up its own members in the fullness of what it has received from its founding and gone on continually reinterpreting through its history. This process can hardly avoid being an educative one. Jesus saw himself as a teacher and the Church tries to carry on his activity of teaching, across huge historical and cultural transformations, to those who by faith are more or less disposed to attend to it. This activity of teaching or catechesis, as it is articulated in several documents since the Second Vatican Council, is a full-blooded endeavour. It aims at an opening of the heart, a deepening of understanding and knowledge, and a reorientation of life experience. In the words of *Catechesi tradendae*, it has an 'entirely pastoral perspective', attempting to bring the student 'organically into the life of the Church', which is a life of liturgy and sacraments as well as of witness.[5]

I expect other speakers at the conference, more theologically informed than I, to develop, and perhaps to correct, what I have just briefly outlined. My particular task requires me to return immediately to the question of the school – which, you will remember, I stepped back from for a moment in order to make this outline. We return to it as a public institution – at least to the extent that, though privately owned and managed, it is heavily funded and in important respects regulated by the State; and also, in a sense which we are perhaps now in a better position to analyse, a *Catholic* institution. The fact that it is a Catholic school means that the Church sees it as a suitable medium in which to carry out the catechetical task that I have just briefly outlined. There is of course no necessary connection between catechesis and schooling – not just because the state might well refuse to allow such a connection but also because the Church itself might choose to carry out its catechetical work entirely outside the school, finding or developing other structures as more fitted to this task. But what are the implications of the present policy of inserting this work within the school – I mean not the obvious implication that, with this policy in place, other structures are likely to remain undeveloped but rather the implications for the school itself? Given the robust notion of it that I have briefly outlined, catechesis can never be simply one element among others in the school programme. It is expected rather to inform and in some sense to integrate the whole programme. The Council's *Declaration on Christian Education* speaks of the Catholic school as striving 'to relate all human culture eventually to the news of salvation so that the light of faith will illumine the knowledge which students gradually gain of the world, of life and of mankind', and it speaks also of the need 'to create for the school community an atmosphere enlivened by the Gospel spirit of freedom and love'.[6] Here we are dealing with a notoriously controversial issue which figured very prominently in the great battles of the nineteenth century between the British administration and the Irish Catholic bishops – as well as in some quite public debates between the bishops themselves.[7] And that it has lost none of its explosive potential is evident from the fact that, according to recent newspaper reports, a court action invoking the Constitution is pending in relation to it. Without reference to this particular case, I shall make a few comments on it.

Any religion worth its salt will make absolute demands – notwithstanding the incapacity or unwillingness of most, if not all, of the faithful to make a commensurate response. This absoluteness ('Thou shalt love the Lord thy God with thy whole heart ...') cannot but be a source of tension in a person's life and in the community and history to which she or he belongs. It is a matter of infinite regret that it has found extreme expression not only in the martyrdom of justly remembered believers but also in the violent persecution of unjustly forgotten non-believers. Whatever the terrible aberrations, however, it is relevant to note here that the Catholic tradition is one which at its best is committed to reconciliation with and not suppression of the great intellectual achievements of each age. To be sure, what might be termed the over-pious mind is easily disconcerted by the untrammelled intellect and even more, perhaps, by the uninhibited imagination. It does make a difference, though, that Catholicism is not a fundamentalist religion and, whatever the tensions, aspires to an integral humanism. Any attempt to violate the integrity of different branches of knowledge or to distort them on behalf of a higher theological truth ought therefore to be open to criticism and correction from within the Catholic tradition itself. But this is a point that I shall not dwell on, both because of the danger of special pleading and also because of the huge and controversial matters of historical and theological judgement which it opens up.

The issue at hand – the non-compartmentalised nature of catechesis, its claim to pervade the whole curriculum – can be addressed more strictly from the viewpoint of philosophy of education. Integration of knowledge may be judged to be a good thing at any level of education. It is difficult to achieve at the more advanced levels when subject specialisation has become the norm. And yet there is hardly a greater need in higher education than good inter-disciplinary work; and this not only for the sake of the unity and expansiveness of mind that Newman extolled but also because it is required by most of the really serious problems that beset us. If integration at the higher level is a desirable though difficult ideal, at the lower level it is not only desirable but almost unavoidable. Even if one disapproved of what is called the integrated curriculum in the primary school, with young children I don't think one could, if one tried, teach any subject as hermetically sealed from every other subject. Not only catechesis but the teaching of other subjects too, and ultimately the child, would suffer from the attempt. This fact creates severe legal difficulty – in that it makes it hard to see how a child's constitutional right to opt out of the religious instruction of a school can actually be exercised without requiring her to opt out of the whole programme – thereby violating another right guaranteed to each child by the constitution, namely the right to attend a school in receipt of state funding.[8] To this legal-constitutional problem (precipitated, it may be said, by the hardly avoidable reality, if not by adherence to the principle, of curricular integration) it is not easy to see a satisfactory solution – short, of course, of excluding catechesis altogether from the school; but this is a prospect that can hardly be deemed satisfactory by believers – or, perhaps, by non-believers who are sensitive to the educational needs of believers.

THE CONCEPT OF AN EDUCATIONAL ETHOS

When the religious character of a school in this wider sense is discussed, a concept that is often introduced is that of the 'Catholic ethos'. What is one to make of this concept? Although the word 'ethos' has a somewhat effete ring, the concept itself is bolstered by recent work in both educational theory and philosophy. A notion which has gained currency in educational literature is that of the 'hidden curriculum'.[9] This is what is learned tacitly and unreflectively just by participation in a particular kind of situation or environment; it may not be advertised or even adverted to as part of the official agenda, or overt curriculum, and yet it comprises attitudes and dispositions that are all the more deeply and enduringly internalised for being carried through the medium of interaction rather than being stated as explicit messages; to a great extent it is what one remembers – or, perhaps better, what onc is – after one has forgotten almost everything else that one learned at school. If one wants to know what the ethos of an institution is, one should try to discover what is learned in this 'hidden' way through belonging to it or participating in its life.

The more philosophical dimension of the notion of ethos emerges from the critique of an overly rationalistic conception of knowledge and an overly individualistic conception of the self that has been under way in much of the best philosophy of the past few decades. There has been a steady dismantling of the positivism that had been so much in ascendancy since the nineteenth century and which not only made religion appear as an unenlightened throwback but also, it can be argued, misconstrued the nature of knowledge, even – indeed one might say especially – of scientific knowledge. The positivist picture, which was itself ultimately a working out of Cartesian assumptions – depicted knowledge as the achievement of a detached, context-free subject, inhabiting a kind of sterilised zero-point, from which, just by attending to unbiassed evidence and, in the case of the scientist, by using the entirely neutral arsenal of procedures made available by the 'scientific method', he could reach objective truth. The different picture which many philosophers now paint is of knowledge – even science – as a communal, tradition-bound activity that always operates within a matrix of assumptions and commitments; this matrix, or paradigm (to use the term popularised by Thomas Kuhn)[10] is not itself easily seen because it is through it that one sees everything that one does see. It frames one's questions, interpretations and judgements; from behind one's back, as it were, it conditions what one is prepared to admit as interesting problems or what one will count as satisfactory solutions. It has become so ingrained in one's habitual way of construing the world one can scarcely recognise what is in fact the case: that it did once require commitment and even a certain kind of faith to enter it. It did so, that is, for the first bold spirits who opened it up and as it were made the leap into it – so that eventually, by a process of initiation and assimilation, it has come down to others as the familiar foot-step of their minds.[11]

Now this revised picture of *knowledge* can be complemented with a correspondingly revised picture of the *person*. A person may be understood not as the disembodied ego, the enclosed consciousness, of the Cartesian picture; or, rather, if there is a person who is self-enclosed and isolated this very isolation can itself be understood as socially constructed – as the product of damaged relationships and an inadequately nurturing community. The self that one becomes, even the personal conscience that one develops and the relative autonomy or independence that one achieves, all happen within a nexus of relationships, a web of interdependency that binds one in all kinds of invisible ways to others. And of course it is not only one's reconnection with others that has to be achieved but also one's reconnection with one's body, with the whole affective and symbolic side of one's nature that has been so discredited (though it has in so many ways taken its revenge) by the official ideology of 'Reason' – an ideology which is still entrenched in most of our curricula and institutional arrangements.[12] If some good recent philosophy has revealed this more holistic perspective, it may be said that it has been restoring much of what was already stored in the proverbial wisdom of such phrases as *'is ar scáth a chéile a mhairean na daoine'* or in the core idea of the doctrine of original sin (or original blessing, if you will) – that we are all inextricably implicated together in a common human condition. But this restoration has in fact been hard won in reflection and, as I shall try to show in a moment, is all the time being threatened in practice. In fact it is precisely as a *critique* of the dominant tendencies of modern society that it has been articulated.

Returning now from this philosophical excursus, how are we to relate it with ethos as something that might in an important sense characterise a school? If knowledge is the sort of reality and, more importantly, if the person is the kind of being that I have suggested, then the sort of environment in which knowledge can develop and the person can flourish is one which provides a kind of subsoil in which roots can be sunk without having to be all the time taken up for inspection. It is one in which people can be jointly engaged in practices that are themselves sustained by living traditions. It is one in which a person can find an identity by having something to identify with or be committed to: something that is sufficiently challenging to ensure that if he/she rejects it then at least he/she will have gained something substantial, will have acquired some character, through the very rejection. Subsoil, practices, tradition, identity, character; these are the realities to be associated with an ethos in good order in a school. Perhaps certain games are the best exemplars of this kind of good order and, far from looking down on these games, perhaps we should only lament that not all children are disposed to become absorbed in them, and that, even for those who are, so many other school activities rarely if ever take on this same game-like quality.[13]

I have used the phrase 'good order', then, because an ethos may of course be in bad order: its practices may not engage or integrate people's energies. It may involve them in discontinuous tasks that are only externally or instrumentally rewarding – if rewarding at all. It may not be informed by tradition but only artificially propped up by traditionalism (tradition, someone has well said, is the living faith of the dead, whereas traditionalism is the dead faith of the living). Or it may make no pretence to any connection at all with the past, simply reacting to whatever is the latest fashion or most powerful pressure – and thereby forming a rootless character and conferring an identity that is shallow and precarious.

And now we come back to the question: what is a Catholic ethos? In terms of the foregoing, the answer seems clear: one in which the Catholic tradition is alive; which means that it not only challenges young people but is challenged by them and thus kept alive. It is one where students can engage in the kind of practices that offer a fair chance that, in acquiring a character or identity, they will be significantly affected by Christian understandings. And here I make a few qualifications. First, it is neither possible nor desirable to have only Christian voices in the conversation to which young people are introduced through their education; this is the conversation that they internalise as their own mental and psychic life; it is made up of many different and dissonant voices through which they must find and modulate their own voice. It should not be expected that, among these voices, the Christian one will always be the loudest; it may be enough if it remains insistent. And this brings me to the second point: the notion of ethos itself, as I sketched it, suggests a dimension of hiddeness and of time. It is not so much the overt behaviour of the present as the long-term orientation that is important; and this may be simply an openness that may not even be recognised until, after the difficult passage to adulthood has been negotiated, it comes to fruition. And a final qualification, potentially radical in its implications: if one sees education in this non-functionalist way, it is all the more necessary that the freedom of the pupil should be respected and promoted. To violate this freedom is *ipso facto* to forfeit a genuinely educational outcome of the endeavours of a teacher or of a school. While this is a fundamental principle of *education*, it need not be seen as enjoining something external on *religious* education; for the Gospel spirit which is to inform Christian education is itself, as we have seen, a spirit of 'freedom and love'. Still, in something as intimately personal as religious belief, the stakes are as high as they can be. Working out the implications for school practices of seeing freedom as a necessary (though not sufficient) condition of catechesis calls for continuous reflection and review.[14] This is all the more urgent when, even if some parents have some choice with respect to schools, for pupils – who, especially at the senior post-primary level, may dissent from their parents' religious viewpoints – school attendance is effectively compulsory. Given the realities of contemporary schooling, the tension here is sure to be very great. Whether it can be creatively and honestly resolved within the school – or calls, rather, for a displacement of catechesis in the strict sense (though not necessarily instruction about religions or indeed many of the themes that are covered in present catechetical programmes) from the school altogether – is a question which must, I believe, remain open.

Related to, but distinct from, respect for the pupil's freedom is concern for the integrity of the object-domain of catechesis. This latter issue arises perhaps even more acutely in the primary school where children are introduced to the sacraments of reconciliation, the eucharist and confirmation. Is the integrity of the sacraments as received by some pupils in jeopardy when virtually all children go for confession, first communion or confirmation because they are in second or in sixth class? Increasing numbers of parents with children in Catholic schools are not practising Catholics themselves; but very few, it seems, withhold their children from reception of the sacraments. What kind of communication is the teacher expected to establish with the child, however, when there is no communication between the Church and the parent? It might be said that the Gospels make it plain that Jesus saw the kingdom as very much (indeed, perhaps uniquely) available to children; and that in this as in other areas it is alright that parents should face a challenge to themselves through their children's education.[15] Whatever the truth of these two propositions, however (and there is more unqualified truth in the first than in the second), the question must remain: without support for it in the home, and with the whole group context that necessarily obtains in the school, will the reception of the sacraments by some children – the best efforts of teachers notwithstanding – not be merely ritualistic? Or rather, since ritual is intrinsic to the sacraments, what needs to be asked is whether what the children experience is the religious reality which the sacrament is designed to make present or simply a secular initiation rite – an early stage, perhaps, of the debutante culture. If it be granted that there is a real problem here, the solution does not lie in simply expecting that parents should have the 'courage of their convictions' nor, I believe, in the Church's setting more stringent conditions for participation in the sacraments; it lies, rather, in creating a context where parents will have no ground for fearing that their non-participating children will suffer from painful exclusion among their peers. But this opens up issues, beyond the Catholic school and the integrity of the sacraments, concerning overall school provision in relation to parental wishes; and in this latter context I shall return to it later.

THE EFFECTIVE DETERMINANTS OF ETHOS

Having identified a tension in Catholic education from the point of view of freedom as a principle of education, I shall now try to show how this tension is greatly exacerbated by the function that the school has come to fulfil in an advanced industrial society and ultimately by the ethos of that society itself. The school's main social role has become one of equipping and selecting people for jobs – or for no jobs. As well as providing them with knowledge and skills, the school is to shape a character that will be adapted to the routines of the society it serves. The key mechanism here is the centralised, standardised examination which, far from being merely a terminal assessment, comes to condition, because of the high stakes that ride on it, a great deal of the teaching/learning process right down to the senior classes in some primary schools. Given the kind of medium that the school thus becomes, what attitudes or character traits are effectively learned – even if they are not overtly stated in any syllabus? Among them, surely, are dispositions to competitiveness, individualism and instrumental achievement. I say instrumental achievement because students are discouraged by the exam culture from learning to engage in practices or to prize certain competencies or excellences for their own sake, or to define problems or goals of their own, and learn rather how to satisfy external criteria, becoming ingenious – and often cynical – in tailoring their efforts for the sake of rewards that lie beyond. I do not claim that teachers never succeed in breaking through this culture or that superb instances of teaching do not occur.[16] Nor do I deny that schools differ significantly in some respects even while belonging to the same overall system.[17] I do not claim, either, that assessment has not an important place in school; or (a very different proposition) that rational and just procedures of selection are not necessary after school when, in areas of employment, training or higher education, there are more candidates than available positions; or that an acceptable alternative to our present system could be easily achieved. I do want to suggest, though, that in general this examination system has a hugely determinative, and in important respects malign, effect on the quality of teaching and learning. This is the case because of its power to dictate the terms in which educational success is defined – the success of pupils, teachers and schools. This definition may not accord with the philosophy or wishes of many teachers, pupils or parents but, given its overwhelming structural power in the life of school, it is extraordinarily difficult to make other definitions prevail against it.[18] Such definitions tend, rather, to be consigned to phantasy, utopianism or free-floating resentment.

This ethos – which I am suggesting is the dominant one in our post-primary sector – should be related, however briefly, to the wider ethos of our society. There are two features of this wider ethos that I especially want to mention. The first is the growing hegemony of scientific–technical reason, the tendency to treat significant issues of our lives as problems that can be objectified and for which the appropriate experts can devise the most efficient and economic solutions. More and more areas of life – politics, business, communications, education and even family life itself – are being subjected to this kind of rationalisation; and as this happens, as the realm of Technique expands, the realm of what may be called Practice attenuates. Practices are still vitally connected to traditions that are alive in all kinds of tacit and nuanced ways in practitioners; these are traditions that offer some strong definition of the good or goal of the practice and at the same time allow scope for reflection and discussion that may re-define the goal, as well as for personal judgement about how to attain it in concrete situations. As practices in this sense are increasingly eliminated or marginalised, as social processes become more administered – more subject to technical imperatives claiming to be value-free – people become more de-politicised, spectators of a public scene in relation to which they can feel little responsibility or personal power.[19]

That's the first feature of our wider societal ethos – what I shall call *technicism*. The second feature I want to mention is closely related to it. With the supposed value-neutrality of the technicist culture and the decline of a public space – where there is a real substantive political debate – what are called 'values' migrate to the private sphere which, separated more and more from the public sphere, is the sheltered area within which the individual is now to find her real fulfilment. A rhetoric of autonomy – and self-realisation – can easily be invoked to put an ethical gloss on the bleakness of the technicist society. While this society requires its school system to turn out competent and well-adapted functionaries, it can make an appearance of offering them something more human or personal in the sphere of 'autonomy' and of 'values'; and it can be aided in this by a trend that conceives the task of moral education as that of simply helping individuals to clarify and choose their own values.[20] From the tendency of public space to become morally vacuous, however, the autonomous individual is in danger of becoming an empty individual: an autonomous individual is one who chooses her own values, and values are what are chosen by the autonomous individual. Given the weightlessness of such values, autonomy can cash out as the freedom to pursue one's self-interest. And politics can be reduced to operating a framework within which this pursuit can occur, while at the same time providing a safety mechanism to stabilise it – the welfare system, aided periodically in Ireland's case by emigration. Nor need this be changed much by two value-terms that do have some public credibility – justice as a form of fairness, and equality. For what is to be equalised or made fair is access to the opportunities and resources through which people can increase their own advantage. This idea of justice and equality keeps in place, and in fact legitimates, the basic element of competition which remains at the core of our society. Aggressive but fair pursuit of self-interest is the name of the game and a great deal of politics consists in over-seeing the ground rules that enable it to go on.

The picture I have just sketched is a 'totalistic' one and, though it is supported at a philosophical level by a wide and diverse range of literature, it will no doubt seem to many to be overdrawn.[21] It hardly docs justice to the spontaneity, exuberance and generosity that break through in all kinds of haphazard ways – often in the most trying circumstances – to give buoyancy to our whole way of life. Nor does it seem to take into account genuine and widespread concern (expressed in ordinary moral intuitions and local practical initiatives as well as at the level of theoretical discourse and international institutions) about, for example, the environment, world poverty and the proliferation of armaments; or more enlightened attitudes to gender, race and the proper nurture of children. The irrepressibility of the human spirit is not of course in doubt, nor, for that matter, do I question the moral insights of specifically modern consciousness. Neither do I want to deny that the former can always be relied upon to manifest itself in schools (only too much, as teachers must often feel!) while the latter, too, have increasingly been assimilated into educational practices over the past few decades. It is a matter, though, of how much all of this may be vulnerable to (even though, paradoxically, in the case of the latter it may also be made possible by) the fundamental mode of organisation of our society. The question is whether these impulses will be given effective space only so long as they act as a lubricant or palliative within the overall technicist system, or at least do not present any real threat to its relentless expansion. And this question, posed thus at a very general level, finds a more specific expression in the field of education, when one notices how the school's complicity in the system (via the examination mechanism) is not really threatened by the child-centred expansiveness of the official primary school curriculum, but that, on the contrary, the latter is always in danger of being rolled back – especially, as the past decade has shown us, when a time of economic difficulty coincides with the dominance of a political ideology which makes no attempt to assuage, but rather makes a virtue of embracing, the technicist logic.

OPTIONS FOR DISCUSSION

What has emerged in the two preceding sections is that 'ethos' is not a rarefied 'extra' that some schools might seek to cultivate on a discretionary basis but rather an unavoidable characteristic of any school; and that Catholic schools, at least at post-primary level, are subject to conditions which must make it very difficult to sustain a Catholic ethos. It should be noted that the tensions I have identified do not just derive from my analysis of the relation between school and society; they arise, rather, when this analysis is brought up against the Church's own professed vision of education and at the same time the necessity of freedom in education (which the Church's vision anyhow incorporates) is kept in focus. I shall now present for discussion, in very clipped terms, three (not mutually exclusive) options with regard to Catholic education, which seem to me to arise if the thrust of what has been presented is at all persuasive. Each of these options (and there is also of course a fourth option – to try to maintain the *status quo*) is problematic in ways which I shall not explore in the paper but which may be clarified in the subsequent discussion.

1 Step back and ask quite radically what a Catholic education might look like. Define it in a strong sense, work out its

practical implications and offer it to parents – knowing full well that it will imply stronger commitments and more painful choices for them. There will no longer be the luxury of an education that is simultaneously Catholic and offers such a high probability of what has been called 'the right peers and the right points'. Implication: fewer Catholic schools but ones of greater integrity. Question: would this be a form of withdrawal that is appropriate to a sect but not to a church?[22]

2 Cut one's losses with schools altogether; abandon them as suitable institutions for carrying out catechesis (the Church was able to baptise Greek philosophy but should stop trying to baptise the modern school!). This would entail a radical reappraisal of the parish structure with a view to creating alternative ways of doing what the schools have been supposed to do. (Religion, of course, might still find a place on the school curriculum – perhaps even as a subject in itself – but in a non-catechetical context, simply as a significant element in western, and indeed non-western, cultures.) And it would mean taking more seriously the notion, to which the Church is officially committed, that *adult* catechesis is the 'principal form of catechesis'.[23]

3 Not abandon schools – but not accept them in their present reality either. Put resources into challenging in every way possible the dominant ethos I have described. This would involve an explicitly political role – building alliances on a wide front with whatever groups or individuals are, for similar reasons, opposed to the present ethos. In theological language, it would involve looking to schools as loci not so much of catechesis as of evangelisation in the broad sense. It would also involve asking whether energy is well spent in fighting to retain control in management terms – when, on the above analysis, having this control still leaves the Church so powerless to do what, in terms of its own professed policy (in some of the documents I have quoted), it wants to do.

PARENTS AND SCHOOLING

These options, and the tensions to which they are possible responses, have been articulated within the Catholic perspective that was explicitly introduced earlier. Since that introduction, the perspective of the democratic polity (which had been briefly developed earlier) has been left in abeyance – with a tacit assumption that Catholic schools can be inserted into it via an appeal to parents' rights. This assumption needs to be examined more closely, however, and in doing so now, I shall resume and explore more fully the implications of the democratic perspective.

I have already noted that the Church's appeal to parents' rights is double-edged: it might lead precisely to its forfeiting much of its power in the educational system. Here two issues ought to be distinguished, however. One is empirical and pertains to what parental preferences actually are, what mechanisms can be put in place to ascertain them and, given demographic and economic realities, what institutional provisions can be made to cater for them. But undercutting these empirical matters is a quite distinct issue of principle: irrespective of what parental preference may be (and therefore of how strong or weak, concentrated or diluted, parental support may be in different areas for Catholic schools), how far can these *preferences* with regard to their own children's education be translated into *rights* with respect to public policy on schooling?

Prescinding for the moment from the second of these issues, I shall make a few points in relation to the first one. Parents have not, in general, been organised to found or manage schools or to negotiate with the public authority on educational policy.[24] Instead, what might be called the 'official' Church (bishops, parish clergy and religious priests, sisters and brothers) has acted as intermediary or broker, being granted the school franchise, as it were, by government and, at the same time, possessing sufficient moral authority with parents to be able, on the whole, to gain their support in exercising it. This arrangement has evolved out of an earlier situation in which the official Church was more active in education, in its own right, providing schooling to the young, with little or no support from the State, at a time when the latter had not assumed the responsibility, and in any case lacked the resources, to make comprehensive educational provision. The Church's priority has been to ensure that religion as an element or, better, a dimension, of education was adequately catered for. Its preferred way of doing this has been to take upon itself, with the State's support, the burden of establishing, owning and managing schools, and staffing them with principals and teachers not only of religion but of other subjects as well. At a purely empirical level, however, two distinct but complementary changes now make this strategy highly problematic: a very significant decline in the human resources at the disposal of the official Church and, at the same time, a very significant expansion in the scope and depth of educational provision through an increasing commitment by the State to education as an area of priority. As the Church's historical stake in education changes – if for no other reason than it itself is no longer able to maintain it – the question of new schooling arrangements, and of the place of religion within them, naturally arises and this of course is a question not only for the Church but also for parents and for the State.

Even if parents have not been active partners in education at the structural level, still they, too, have been subject to changes which are clearly of direct relevance here. In the first place, many parents – a continually growing number, it seems likely – though brought up as Catholics, no longer regard themselves as such, and are alienated from the Church in various degrees from benign indifference to strong hostility. (A great many find themselves uncertain and conflicted, with their received faith no longer plausible in everyday experience,[25] while residual loyalties are often stirred by the background presence, as grandparents, of their own parents – and they are meanwhile confronted with decisions in relation to their children's upbringing which they feel uncomfortably unready to make.) From the Church's point of view, it must be important that these people should not have grounds for regarding their children as conscripts in Catholic schools – for the well-being of these schools themselves and also in virtue of the Church's professed position on religious liberty. But, whatever the Church's attitude, the State, surely, has the duty of ensuring that schools congruent with the beliefs of these parents are available to their children. Second, there are Catholic parents who wish their children to be educated in a school which will be attended also by children of other religions, or of no religion, and where, in an ecumenical spirit, a positive value will be put on all of these different backgrounds of belief; such a spirit may itself be seen as forming a valuable educational ethos – one, moreover, which need not exclude, in close consultation with parents, arrangements for separate instruction of groups of children in particular religious traditions. Such schools have emerged at primary level in Ireland over the past two decades, largely in response to initiatives of local communities – communities which have in turn been strengthened by carrying through these initiatives, often against considerable odds.[26] The question must be, however, whether the State has not a duty to encourage, or at least to facilitate, these initiatives by lessening the odds against them.[27]

CIVIL AUTHORITY AND THE ROLE OF THE SCHOOL

It is at this point that we can profitably take up the second issue mentioned above, namely the issue of principle. I introduced this issue a few moments ago in terms of parents' rights. The rights-claims in question here are directed primarily to the State and so the issue is also one of defining the nature and scope of the State's role in schooling – and hence, too, of the role of the school itself in society. That the State in fact exercises huge control over schooling is evident: the content of curricula, the organisation of examinations, the certification of teachers, the fixing of the minimum school-leaving age, the determination of teacher–pupil ratios and the setting of broad guidelines on school discipline (e.g. the proscribing of corporal punishment) are among the more important policy matters on which the State, albeit in consultation with the educational 'partners', is the final arbiter. What concerns us here, however, is to identify the matters on which the State ought to defer to the wishes of parents or, more precisely, to define the normative basis for State policies which do not so defer. An obvious point is that parents do not have absolute rights over their children – quite simply because the children themselves have certain basic rights; and so one ground for the State's prerogatives here is qua guarantor or protector of children's rights, in cases where the latter may be deemed (ultimately by the courts) to be violated or seriously endangered by the parents. Some might take the view that the initiation of young children into a religious faith is itself a violation of the child's right to freedom of conscience. It would of course be an extraordinarily intrusive state which would try to outlaw this activity within the homes of citizens. But what about the schools? Will a State not exclude certain practices from schools on the grounds that, though appropriate (or at least tolerable) as part of *upbringing* in the privacy of the home, they are not legitimate as part of *public education*? And might the teaching of religion be deemed to be such a practice? An affirmative answer might be given to this question on the basis that the teaching of religion, at least when it is conducted within a catechetical frame, is necessarily indoctrinatory and not, therefore, to be countenanced in a State-supported school.[28] However, although catechesis certainly can be, and perhaps often is, indoctrinatory, I do not believe that the charge of indoctrination can be made to stick against catechesis *per se* (as distinct from corrupt forms of it). I say this mainly because of my belief that the ground from which this charge is typically made is philosophically unsustainable. My reasons for thinking this were touched on earlier, when I sketched a philosophical background to the notion of ethos; but developing the argument lies beyond the scope of this present paper.

Even if appeal is not made to the notion of 'indoctrination', other considerations might weigh with a state in its attitude to religion in schools and in particular to religious affiliation as a basis for establishing and maintaining separate schools. Quite apart from economic ones, broad civic or political considerations might affect a state's schooling policy – and in such a way as to constrain the choices of parents. (The 'bussing' policy of US governments serves as a good example here of a civic–political commitment – to positive action for racial integration – having direct and, to some of those affected, unpalatable consequences for schooling policy.) The view might simply be taken that a modern pluralist democracy is committed to separation of Church and State, and that State functions – and hence education in State-funded schools – must, therefore, be irreducibly secular. Rights to religious practice and indeed to religious education – in the home, in the parish or even in private schools – may be protected by State laws; but State-funded schools must be committed to a public culture that is not determined by particular religious beliefs or by differences among them. Sometimes, this position is criticised as a form of neutralism which is morally vacuous. But it need not be so (in the sense intended – for of course no culture can ever really be neutral). To the contrary, it might be motivated precisely by a concern for civic morality, which might be seen as an indispensable element in public education, not to be left dependent on religious instruction (and, in fact, requiring special attention at a time of declining religious belief and practice). And it might be added that, though this is an issue for all states, it has a peculiar salience in ones that are former colonies – and especially, perhaps, in ones where the idea of the 'nation' has been demythologised to the extent that is has been in Ireland over the past quarter of a century.

In response to this view it might be said that although the State quite rightly assumes some responsibility for the viability of the civic culture, the latter is not something that can be conjured up by policy decision. It can scarcely exist without a tradition or, rather, a confluence of different traditions. And if, for historical reasons, Ireland has lacked some of the elements that have gone into the formation of strong civic cultures in other European countries, the question may arise as to whether the Irish State has the moral capital to justify it in evacuating from its educational system, on secularist principle, the moral resources of its major religious traditions. A negative answer here seems to be implied by J.J. Lee when he suggests that in contemporary Ireland religion is 'the main barrier between a reasonably civilised civil society and the untrammelled predatory instincts of individual and pressure-group selfishness, curbed only by the power of rival predators ... If religion were to no longer fulfil its historic civilising mission as a substitive for internalised rules of civic responsibility, the consequences for the country no less than for the Church could be lethal.'[29]

Lee's position here may cause unease if it is taken as prescriptive for the New Ireland. But as descriptive of the Ireland we have known it has a lot of truth; and it provides a chastening invitation to consider the challenge that faces us as a society. With the decline of institutional religion the civil authority will not just find the ecclesiastical voice less intimidating; it will also have to recognise the need to make more transparent to young citizens what their country has to offer them, why its laws and institutions deserve their respect, and what obligations they have towards their fellow citizens. It will, in other words, have to ensure that they are educated in that moral and civic virtue ('internalised rules of civic responsibility') for which religion up to now has been a 'substitute'. We should realise, though, just how formidable a task this is – and that there may be a strong interest in finding some *other* substitute to obviate the need to really tackle it. For tackling it properly, we might discover, would open up many sore issues. What would it involve, for instance, in a school serving an area where in 80 per cent of the homes no parent has a job, where transport and recreational facilities are inadequate and where there is a huge reliance on social services which are manifestly unable to cope? What account of society and of their own place in it is to be offered to students in such a school? Is it one that can both engage their critical capacities and at the same time make plausible any sense of genuine social justice and solidarity? I raise these questions not because I know any satisfactory answers to them but simply in order to point out: a) that a serious civic education would go beyond unproblematic information to embrace attitudes, convictions and ways of acting, and that it could not avoid controversy and division (not that it would itself be necessarily divisive but rather that it would bring more into focus already existing divisions); and b) that it does not then provide a clear basis for excluding the teaching of religion from the school on the grounds of *its* being divisive (albeit in a different way). In fact, there may be pressure to exclude both this kind of civic/political education and catechesis from the school, and for much the same reasons – that both of them are dysfunctional in that they open spaces for reflection (which other subjects too are in their own ways capable of creating but which tend to be swamped by the examination pressures to which these subjects must submit). Viewed in this perspective, catechesis might be more likely to be left in the school – being seen as less threatening than a critical programme of social/political education. But this judgement on catechesis may prove mistaken in that the kind of faith which survives into the future may be one which will not easily be a substitute for anything else – least of all for a sense of responsibility.

I should acknowledge that there is a significant difference between the kind of divisiveness that a civic–political education might bring into focus and the kind which is maintained through denominational schooling, and that the above remarks only point out the difficulties of adequately replacing catechesis – without providing any principled argument for retaining it. We should look more closely, though, at the relation between religion and the State. In speaking of the State, we need not suppose that it is a perfect representative of civil society – any more than, as we have just seen, this society itself is securely harmonious. The modern State bureaucracy can concentrate power in the hands of a few decision-makers, as well as respond to powerful pressure groups, in ways that make it only very imperfectly accountable to those whom it is supposed to serve. (Democracy can be distorted by the State apparatus no less than Christianity can be disfigured by the institutional Church.) The practical/moral upshot of this advertence to the fallibility of the State, of course, is 'eternal vigilance' on the part of citizens – and not any devolution of State powers to the Church. Still, what we need to clarify here are the implications *for education* of a separation of Church and State. Although education is indeed an inescapably political matter, perhaps we should recognise an important difference between the imperatives that govern politics in the wider sense and those that govern education specifically. Must the school system be treated on all fours with the legal system – in the sense that just as one set of laws binds indifferently all citizens, so one type of school must be indifferently available to all pupils? An upshot of pluralism at the legislative level is that it commits a society at this level to what has been called a 'thin' notion of the good. While this 'thin' or 'procedural' notion of the public good may be desirable at a constitutional/legal level, ought education be open to 'thick' or 'substantive' goods – substantive enough, in different cases, to embrace particular religious traditions?[30] Is education as a humanising activity weakened if engagement with such substantive goods is foreclosed – to the ultimate loss of civil society itself? To provide for substantively rich versions of education in this way, it may be noted, would not entail setting aside procedural principles; for the latter would still be necessary in deciding on equitable and non-discriminatory ways of making such provision, and of course the State would still retain considerable regulative powers. The basic assumption, however, would not be that every school must be congenial to all citizens but rather that, subject to (mainly negative) regulations, all citizens should have a congenial school convenient to them. If this is clear enough as a basic principle, its implementation in practice, of course, would present formidable difficulties – especially in an area of low density population with significant religious diversity.

Mention of practical difficulties here gives an opportunity to acknowledge something that determines us in this as in all socio-political and cultural matters: we are not starting from scratch. When talking about traditions, we should not forget that schools themselves have traditions and life stories. A school, for instance, in which there has been a long continuity of commitment and service, given perhaps over several generations (whether by a religious community or by a local 'moral' community), is not something that should be expected to change its identity with ease. When discussing the matter on the level of principle – as I am doing in this paper – one can easily slip into the illusion that schools are like counters in a board game – easily convertible and disposable. But the very historicity and particularity of what we are always concerned with in human affairs should itself be taken as a matter of principle: it tells us something important about the fundamental constitution of the realities we are dealing with and excludes as a method of dealing with them the approach of the social engineer.[31] And this point need not have conservative implications. On the contrary, it may open up rich and imaginative ways of developing established educational resources. Moreover, it does not just put an onus on those who may be interested in taking over an old institution to be sensitive to the concerns of the present incumbents; equally, it obliges the latter, in relinquishing or disposing of it, to give priority to its educational character.

I am aware of the irony that while I have been making a case for the legitimacy of religion in education through an appeal to pluralist principles, the profile of religious affiliation among the population in Ireland has given us little plurality in practice. The overall thrust of this paper leads me, I believe, to defend the idea of denominational education – notwithstanding the tensions that arise, as I have tried to show, from the realisation of this idea in contemporary society. Nothing I have said, however, impugns the idea of the 'multi-denominational' school (though the term is, perhaps, a misnomer if such a school includes, as it properly might, children of no denomination or of atheist or agnostic parents). On the contrary, I see great merit in such a school if it can find ways to actualise different beliefs and practices, within an overall spirit of mutual understanding and tolerance. Finding an effective vision that can give coherence to the endeavours of all those responsible for it, while maintaining perhaps fundamental differences of perspective, is a very big challenge. It can hardly be denied, however, that attempting to meet it in the kind of society that is now emerging in Ireland is a significant educational undertaking.

THE SCHOOL, 'COMMUNITY' AND TEACHERS

It is often recognised as a strength of denominational schools that they are supported by an explicit commitment on the part of the home and of the local parish community.[32] While the evidence of common-sense and of research suggests that close school-home-community liaison is educationally beneficial, there is hardly much ground for supposing, however, that religious denomination is the only, or even necessarily the strongest, factor that can elicit and sustain such liaison. There is surely much to be said for a school serving a local community. Up to recently, in many parts of the Republic, the local civic community has been, or at least seemed to be, virtually coincident with the Roman Catholic community; and so the Catholic school could be seen not as dividing the community, but rather as benefitting from the existence of an integral geographical community. But with the decline in denominational allegiances this will no longer be the case. A Catholic school will no longer be able to serve or be sustained by the integral community in such an unproblematic way. A multi-denominational school, on the other hand, might aspire to serve this whole community, and might draw sustenance from whatever vibrancy and solidarity exist in it. One does not want to romanticise 'community', of course, or make the word do more work than the reality can bear; for in this, as in other cases, the word becomes fashionable just when the thing itself has become problematic. In some areas, particularly in the larger cities, a school hardly has any community, Catholic or otherwise, into which it can nest; on the contrary it may have to see itself as a potent agency for slowly *creating* community. And Catholic residents (and clergy) of such an area must surely ask themselves whether contributing to a school for the whole community – in which there is real scope for them to make their distinctive contribution count – may not be a better choice than holding out for a school of their own.

Throughout the paper I have spoken of the concerns of parents and children, the Church and the State and, just now, the local community. I have said almost nothing about teachers, however. And yet, without them, nothing that has been said so far can be given any reality. It is not just as vehicles for the interests of other parties, however, that teachers need to be taken into account. They have legitimate concerns of their own which, in this matter, cannot be said to be justly met in our present school structures. No less than parents, there are teachers who profess or practise no religion. What is their lot, however, especially at primary level, when, having come through a denominational system of teacher-education, they must find employment in an almost exclusively denominational school system? An obvious answer is: exile, silence or cunning. Is it defensible that the price to be paid for a stable post in one's chosen profession, or promotion in it, may be some form of suppression or dissembling, if not outright hypocrisy and deception? Pressure in this direction within our system must be considered unjust to individuals and sadly distorting both of education and of religion. Two responses to it seem to be desirable. First, the Catholic school might enlarge its self-understanding so that it could welcome – I say 'welcome' and not just 'tolerate' – a teacher who dissents from the Catholic faith but who shows respect for the religious beliefs and practices in the school. Such a teacher would not be expected to act as a catechist; and is it unrealistic to expect that the school would find a way of honouring her or his conscientiously held convictions and, should she or he so wish, allow the latter explicitly to enrich the educational milieu of the school? The second desirable response transcends the Catholic school. It is simply that the civil authority foster a real plurality of school types. (It should not be forgotten that for many years the vocational school system has offered an alternative type here at post-primary level; and various models in other European countries are certainly worth examining.) Apart from bringing other benefits that we have already seen, such a policy would make available to teachers career options that are more attuned to the actual civil society in which they live.

In attending to the role of teachers here, we should recognise that more is involved than 'teachers' rights'. In fact, what is at stake is the integrity of our whole school system. For whatever 'ethos', denominational or otherwise, may characterise a school, the most powerful way in which it is 'carried', and exercises its educative influence, is through the personal presence of teachers. I had occasion earlier, in the context of the relationship between the state and various religious traditions, to advert to the 'moral resources' of a society. It would be sobering for any society to consider (if a 'society' could consider) just how crucially its moral resources are concentrated in its teachers. With that earlier advertence I wanted to affirm a positive role for different religious traditions in securing the moral well-being of our society. I want to suggest now, however, that, if we read the signs of the times, the most important lines to be got clear may not, after all, be between different religious denominations. Our history has indeed bequeathed a particular educational task to us in relation to the latter – one which I have tried to analyse in this paper. I conclude by pointing out, however, that the scenario which I painted earlier, and which led to my posing three options to Catholic educators, still confronts us as a civil society. Schools face the challenge of participating in huge technological change – without being colonised by an unholy alliance of technical rationality, market culture and acquisitive individualism. The really important task is to ensure, in response to this challenge, that a vision of education as a humanising engagement should be continually renewed in practice. And it may be that denominational lines of division will not be the most significant markers for those who find themselves engaged together in this task.[33]

Notes

1   I make no attempt to consider the educational policies or practices of other Christian Churches in the Republic, or the relationship between religion and education in Northern Ireland; I can only hope that my remarks are not insensitive to either of these realities. When I sometimes use the term 'Catholic' as a stand-in for 'Roman Catholic' or 'Christian' as a stand-in for 'Catholic', I do not of course mean to imply that in either case the two terms are convertible.

2 Broadly speaking, one might say that this is the argument on which the public school system in the United States is founded. Its classic formulation is in the writings of John Dewey (see especially his *Democracy and Education*, New York: MacMillan, 1916); a more recent, very able, elaboration of it is to be found in A. Gutmann, *Democratic Education*, Princeton, NJ: Princeton University Press, 1987.

3 'Declaration on Religious Liberty', art. 5, in Walter M. Abbot (ed.), *The Documents of Vatican II*, London: Geoffrey Chapman, 1967.

4 'Declaration on Christian Education', art. 6, ibid.

5 Pope John Paul II, *Catechesi tradendae* (Catechesis in our Time), Athlone: St Paul Publications, 1979, arts. 23, 24 and 25.

6 'Declaration on Christian Education', art. 8 in Abbot (ed), op cit.

7 See D.H. Akenson, *The Irish Educational Experiment,* London: Routledge and Kegan Paul, 1970, chapters 5 and 6.

8 What I distinguish here as two rights are conflated as one right in art. 44, 2, 4 of the Constitution.

9 A seminal book for the notion of the hidden curriculum is Philip Jackson's *Life in Classrooms,* New York: Holt, Rinehart and Wilson, 1968. Jackson's focus on micro processes in the classroom has since been complemented by more broadly sociological work (e.g. by Robert Dreeban) and, more recently, by critical, neo-Marxist perspectives (see e.g. Kathleen Lynch, *The Hidden Curriculum,* London: The Falmer Press, 1989).

10 See T. Kuhn, *The Structure of Scientific Revolutions*, Chicago: University of Chicago Press, 1970.

11 What I summarise here is a philosophical movement across a wide front – one which is not, I realise, uncontroversial. For an excellent account of it, see R.J. Bernstein, *Beyond Objectivism and Relativism*, Oxford: Basil Blackwell, 1980.

12 A most subtle analyst of the two central themes which I only hint at here, namely intersubjectivity and embodiment, is Maurice Merleau-Ponty. See *Phenomenology, Language and Sociology*, London: Heinemann, 1974 and *The Phenomenology of Perception*, London: Routledge and Keegan Paul, 1969.

13 On the general significance of the game and of play, see H.G. Gadamer, *Truth and Method*, London: Sheed and Ward, 1975, pp. 91–9.

14 'Freedom' is a difficult and contested concept, even apart from questions of how it may properly be attributed to children, what its place can or ought to be in formal education, and how reconcilable it may be with 'authority'. Clarification of these issues is one of the

most essential tasks in the philosophy of education and there is, of course, a considerable literature. While its style is not orthodoxly philosophical, I find especially illuminating Martin Buber's essay, 'Education' in *Between Man and Man*, London: Fontana, 1969.

15 Both of these points are made by Maria Montessori; see *The Secret of Childhood*, London: Sangam Books, 1983.

16 In conversation with third level students over a number of years I have found that their recollections of memorable learning experiences in school relate more often to religion – which is conspicuously not on the examination syllabus – than to any other subject.

17 See D. Hannon and M. Boyle, *Schooling Decisions: The Origins and Consequences of Selection and Streaming in Irish Post-Primary Schools*, E.S.R.I. General Research Series No. 136, Dublin: E.S.R.I., 1987.

18 For interesting data and discussion with regard to teachers' views of examinations, see J. Raven, R. Handy, C. Benson, B. Hannon and E. Henry, *A Survey of Post-Primary Teachers and Pupils, Vol. 1, Teachers' Perceptions of Educational Objectives and Examinations*, Dublin: Irish Association for Curriculum Development, 1975, pp. 65–88.

19 On the distinction here between technique and practice, see my *Back to the Rough Ground: Phronesis and Techne in Modern Philosophy and in Aristotle*, Notre Dame and London: University of Notre Dame Press, in press.

20 I do not mean that clarification should play no role in moral education or that everything that goes under the banner of 'values clarification' is educationally undesirable. That benefits can be derived from imaginative modes of clarification, when they are incorporated within a more substantive pedagogy and based on a more philosophically coherent self-understanding than what is often found in presentations of the values clarification position, is ably argued by Frank Dorr, 'Values Clarification and Relativism: A Response to Jim McKernan', *Oideas*, 34, Samhradh, 1989, pp. 105–117. Pádraig Hogan makes a similarly nuanced case, appealing incidentally to the notion of 'ethos', in 'Can Goodness be Taught?', *Furrow*, Vol. 40, No. 2, Feb, 1989.

21 The literature I have in mind here spans very wide bands of the contemporary philosophical spectrum. Much of it is inspired by the three great 'masters of suspicion', Marx, Nietzshe and Freud (for instance Jürgen Habermas's writings brilliantly develop the work of the earlier generation of the 'Frankfurt School' which synthesised Marxist and Freudian perspecties to deliver a ferocious critique of the

oppressive and self-deceiving tendencies of advanced capitalist societies; and, from a neo-Nietzschean perspective, a hardly less disenchanted picture emerges in the writing of Michel Foucault). On the other hand, from a very different viewpoint – one which tries to rehabilitate pre-modern traditions, specifically the Aristotelian and Thomistic ones – Alasdair MacIntyre argues for the moral bankruptcy of modern Enlightenment culture in several books, including the influential *After Virtue*, London: Duckworth, 1981. For an excellent attempt to come to terms with the negative aspects of modernity – and specifically the two features of it that I have highlighted, viz. technicist hegemony and a hollow individualism – while at the same time developing a more generous account of its positive and genuinely liberating tendencies – see Charles Taylor, *Sources of the Self: The Making of the Modern Identity*, New York: Cambridge University Press, 1989.

22 The distinction between 'sect' and 'church' derives from the work of the theologian Ernst Troeltsch and is interestingly deployed by R. Bellah et al. in analysing the role of religion in the contemporary culture of the United States. See their essay 'Social Science as Public Philosophy' in *Habits of the Heart*, New York: Basic Books, 1985, pp. 333–8.

23 *Catechesi tradendae*, n. 43.

24 Recent exceptions to this, worth mentioning, are the founding of multi-denominational primary schools as well as scoileanna lán-Ghaelacha, at local level and, at national level, the establishment of the National Parents' Council.

25 See the illuminating discussion of 'plausibility structures' in Peter L. Berger, *The Sacred Canopy, Elements of a Sociological Theory of Religion*, New York: Anchor Books, 1969.

26 For an account of the emergence of these schools, which provides a helpful historical context, see Áine Hyland, 'The Multi-denominational Experience in the National School System in Ireland', *Irish Educational Studies*, Vol. 8, No.1, (1989), pp. 89–114.

27 For detailed analysis and practical suggestions on this matter, see Bill Hyland, 'A Very Modest Proposal Regarding the Provision of Public Primary Education', in *Church and State*, No. 38 (Summer 1991). A revised version of this paper, 'The Provision of Primary Education in Public Buildings', was presented to the Irish Educational Studies conference in St Patrick's College, Dublin in April 1991 and is to appear in a forthcoming issue of *Irish Educational Studies*.

28 Although he does not state this position categorically, Desmond Clarke presents an argument which seems designed to persuade a reader to conclude to it, in 'Teaching, Indoctrination and Freedom of Thought', *Oideas*, 30, Earrach 1987, pp. 24–36.

29 J.J. Lee, *Ireland 1912–1985, Politics and Society*, Cambridge: Cambridge University Press, 1989, p. 657.

30 The terms 'thick' and 'thin', in the senses used here, gained currency in moral philosophy through the influence of Clifford Geertz in *The Interpretation of Cultures*, New York: Basic Books, 1973; see e.g. Bernard Williams, *Ethics and the Limits of Philosophy*, Cambridge MA: Harvard University Press, 1985 and Charles Taylor, op. cit. The distinction between them corresponds closely with the distinction between 'procedural' and 'substantive' which, as applied to concepts such as rationality and justice, looms large in contemporary debate in political philosophy between liberals and their 'communitarian' critics. Key texts in this debate, which is, I believe, very pertinent to interpretations of contemporary Irish society, are, on the one side, John Rawls, *A Theory of Justice*, Cambridge MA: Harvard University Press, 1971 and Jürgen Habermas, *Communication and the Evolution of Society*, Boston: Beacon Press, 1979 and, on the other, Michael Sandel, *Liberalism and the Limits of Justice*, Cambridge: Cambridge University Press, 1982 and Robert Bellah et al, op. cit.

31 See Aristotle, *Nicomachean Ethics*, 1, 3; and M. Oakeshott, *Rationalism in Politics and Other Essays*, London: Methuen, 1962.

32 See James S. Coleman and Thomas Hoffer, *Public and Private High Schools: The Impact of Communities*, New York: Basic Books, 1987.

33 This paper is a revised and expanded version of what was presented at the conference in April 1991. Of many friends and colleagues who very generously helped me to prepare it, I must acknowledge in particular John Doyle, Gerry Gaden, Frank Litton and Father Fergal O'Connor, O.P.